Outcomes
in
Process

Outcomes in Process

Setting Standards for Language Use

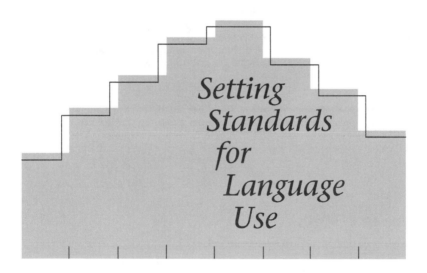

Roseanne Y. DeFabio

Boynton/Cook Publishers
HEINEMANN
Portsmouth, New Hampshire

Boynton/Cook Publishers, Inc.
A subsidiary of Reed Elsevier Inc.
361 Hanover Street
Portsmouth, NH 03801–3912

Offices and agents throughout the world

Library of Congress Cataloging-in-Publication Data

DeFabio, Roseanne Y.
    Outcomes in process : setting standards for language use /
Roseanne Y. DeFabio.
        p.   cm.
    Includes bibliographical references and index.
    ISBN 0–86709–341–2
    1. Language arts—Ability testing.   2. Literacy—Evaluation.
    3. Educational tests and measurements.   I. Title.
    LB1575.D38   1994
    372.6′044—dc20   93-42432
                                                                          CIP

Acquisitions Editor: Peter R. Stillman
Production: Vicki Kasabian
Cover design: Mary Cronin
Printed in the United States of America on acid-free paper
98 97 96 95 94   EB   1 2 3 4 5

For Robert, of course,
and for Daniel and Mary, our best outcomes.

Contents

Acknowledgments

First, I am indebted to all those scholars and educators whose work is listed in the reference section and whose thinking has guided my own teaching of and thinking about language and literature. I have borrowed liberally, and eclectically, from their ideas in order to suggest useful distinctions in the language performance of students at different stages of their development and to describe educational practices that will promote that development. I hope that in doing so I have not lifted some ideas unacceptably out of context. The thinking in this book is based not on the theoretical purity of the academy but in the happy hodgepodge of the classroom where the lions of constructionism lie contentedly with the lambs of expressionism.

Second, I am personally and professionally indebted to the scholar-teachers listed on page 197 who participated in the pilot study and whose thoughtful responses set a direction for continued efforts to develop an outcomes-based language curriculum. They are truly reflective practitioners who bring to their classrooms not only their own examples of excellent language use and their love for language, learning, and literature, but also a wealth of scholarship in the fields of English and English education. I know that my conversations and collaborations with many of them over the last few years have shaped my thinking and strengthened my belief in the power of a community of learners. I am especially grateful to my good friend, Tricia Hansbury-Zuendt, who served as sounding board for every idea as well as critical reader for the section on the pilot study.

Also, I acknowledge gratefully the contribution of my colleagues at the New York State Education Department. The draft of language outcomes that appears in this book was the result of the work of a committee composed of Charles Chew, Alberta Patch-Slegaitis, Jacqueline Marino, Richard Fratta, Phyllis Ross, and me; and several of them reviewed and commented on the pilot study. Much of the thinking in this book on curriculum, instruction, and assessment came out of conversations and collaborations in the department with them and with our colleagues, Coral Crosmann and Paula Rollins.

I am grateful to the members of my family who not only encouraged, prodded, and supported me, but who also read and critiqued the book along the way. My husband, Bob DeFabio, gave me invaluable suggestions for making the content clearer and more accessible to "non-English teachers." My children, Daniel and Mary, cheerfully reversed roles with me and kept me on task with their reminders— "Don't you have a book to write?" Sister Genevieve Conway, my aunt, was coach, reader, and cheerleader throughout the process.

And finally, I am proud and happy to acknowledge the influence of the person who was the inspiration, instigator, reader-critic, and promoter of this book. His influence reminds me of an English teacher I once worked with who believed so strongly in the creative ability of his reluctant students that he kept after them until they produced a volume of delightful poetry and fiction that they entitled *Our Teacher Made Us Do It*. And so, special thanks to my colleague, boss, mentor, and friend, Charles Chew. He made me do it.

Introduction

This book comes out of a gradual and somewhat reluctant recognition of some present realities. One of those realities is the public insistence on national educational standards. In spite of the unwillingness of many educators to contribute to any attempt to compare students across schools, districts, and states, the public demand for an assurance of equity and excellence in the education of all children necessitates thoughtful attention to the definition and public discussion of such standards.

Another reality is that the concept of local control of education is changing as a result of the mobility and interrelatedness of our society and the concern for consistency across districts and states. The "village" in which today's students will live and work is not only a national but a global village, involving all of its members in events far removed from the neighborhoods of their childhood and the experiences of their parents and teachers. If ever there was a world in which people could expect that their children would grow up and live in the same manner as their parents and grandparents (and maybe such a world never did exist), that is not the world we live in now. We live in a world in which children cannot be expected to grow up and live where or as their parents live. It is a world in which farmers' sons will not grow up to be farmers, in which housemakers' daughters will not grow up to be housemakers, and, given the political realities of the world, in which even monarchs' children may not grow up to be monarchs. Local communities can no longer set standards for their graduates based on the particular needs of that community; can no longer assume that their children will stay on in that community to continue its economic, political, and social traditions; and can no longer even expect that those economic, political, and social traditions will continue to exist as they know them. Because today's students are growing up in an increasingly sophisticated and interdependent global society requiring very high levels of intellectual and linguistic competence, it is reasonable that a common set of learning outcomes and standards should be set for all students across the nation and that the opportunity to attain those standards should be recognized as the right of every student.

Determining those outcomes and standards should involve all of us who care about education in an ongoing conversation. We will not get it right once for all time; we will be constantly expanding and refining and adjusting our expectations as we learn from one another and from the students themselves. This book is one contribution to that conversation. It comes out of many other conversations I have had with other educators whose influence I acknowledge with gratitude.

Chapter One

Outcomes and Standards That Respect Process

There will be standards: to begin with. The National Council of Teachers of English knows it. Teachers in classrooms know it. School administrators know it. It's been announced on the front page of the *New York Times*, and there can't be more official notice than that.

As educators, we should resign ourselves to the fact that there will be standards. And not just some general standards about what students should know in curriculum areas other than our own. In math and science, standards make sense and fit in with those disciplines. But make no mistake about it: there will be standards in English language arts, standards for describing what students should be able to do with language and how well they should be able to do it after instruction. And someone is going to determine what those standards will be. The question is, who will set them?

Not me, you say. You don't believe in standards. You think it is inappropriate to draw lists of the proficiencies students should demonstrate in language, to put those proficiencies on some sort of continuum from rudimentary to stupendous (or whatever), and to assess each student's language performance according to where it falls on that continuum. It violates what you believe about language as a process. You won't do it.

Well, then someone else will. Someone is going to come up with language outcomes and standards for grading the performance of those outcomes, and those outcomes and standards will be used to guide the curriculum and assessment students will experience.

If you're like many of the English teachers I know, the current discussion of outcomes-based education, new standards, and authentic

1

assessment has produced anxiety. For many educators, an early reaction to the call for the definition of standards to apply to all students was resistance. The deeper we were involved in process curricula, the more uncomfortable we felt with the call to spell out in measurable specifics what we want our students to know and to be capable of at the end of their schooling. But the call does not go away, and most of us have recognized that if there are to be outcomes and standards they should be of our choosing—outcomes and standards reflecting what we believe about language use and learning.

The purpose of this book is to propose some language outcomes that respect process, outcomes that suggest possibilities for language performance as rich and varied, as individual and as social, and as contextualized and as dynamic as the language English teachers encourage and celebrate in our classrooms.

I will start with what we as English teachers have come to know and value about language from our own experience as language users and language instructors by turning to those scholars and researchers whose writings and findings have validated and conceptualized our own experiential knowledge. I will conclude by bringing the concepts and distinctions found in that theory back into the classroom to see if it really matches our experience and helps us to say more clearly what we observe and value about our students' language performance.

Reflections on Personal Experience

In spite of our reluctance as language instructors to specify language outcomes and standards, all of us have internalized standards to allow us to make judgments about language use not only in classrooms but also in everyday situations as well. We have all observed the negative effects produced when we admit to being an English teacher. Suddenly the garrulous dinner partner becomes tongue tied and mumbles embarrassed disclaimers about watching grammar. This perception of English teachers is unfortunate but not all wrong. We love language; we revel in graceful, elegant, and precise language and are repulsed by clumsy, pedestrian, and inexact language. We collect bits of beautiful language, of bon mots, of witticisms, of allusions. We also collect malapropisms, redundancies, oxymorons, and samples of doublespeak. We have our standards.

What are they? At the risk of defeating my purpose before we begin, I'll admit that they are as individual and diverse as our literary responses, as open to interpretation as the most obscure text, as unexamined as our lives. But there are shadows of them in the responses we make to the language performance around us, and there are commonalities that allow us to share with confidence our favorite examples of language triumphs and atrocities.

Try this test. Who are the best fiction writers, poets, essayists, columnists, and letter writers you know of? Who are the best political speakers, stand-up comics, inspirational speakers, and conversationalists? Who are the best critics, analysts of complex exposition, and readers and interpreters of stories and poems?

Our ease at naming someone whose language is exemplary in some category is evidence of internalized standards for those categories. The fact that we identify people more easily when the categories are split up suggests there are significant differences among the categories. Naming the best speaker would be harder if politicians, entertainers, and evangelists were all included in the same category. Therefore, finding the categories to reflect distinctions is an important first step in defining language outcomes.

Let me propose four categories for language related to the functions of language use described by Michael Halliday (1973). In the broadest terms, I designate those categories aesthetic, social, informational, and critical. When those categories or functions of language use are applied to each of the language arts, twelve language outcomes are created.

- reading for aesthetic response
- reading for social interaction
- reading for information and understanding
- reading for critical analysis and evaluation
- writing for aesthetic response and expression
- writing for social interaction
- writing for information and understanding
- writing for critical analysis and evaluation
- listening/speaking for aesthetic response and expression
- listening/speaking for social interaction
- listening/speaking for information and understanding
- listening/speaking for critical analysis and evaluation

Most of us would agree that those twelve statements represent language abilities every person should have, and they have the advantage of being more explicit than the usual language classifications used to describe students' performance. For example, with the above categories I might say that Mandy is an excellent reader, a good writer, and an effective speaker. These categories provide that information, but they also allow us to describe an individual's command of a particular function, such as Myron is an astute critic. But most importantly, these statements describe the language processes that we value. They reflect what real readers, writers, speakers, and listeners do. As educators, we have extensive experience in making judgments about individuals' language use as readers, writers, listeners, and speakers. We have graded students in those areas with confidence, although each of us may have based those grades on different factors. Some instructors value demonstrations of extensive vocabulary and spelling ability on the assumption that the individual who is able to pass rigorous tests in vocabulary and spelling will be able to use those words effectively in speech and writing. The SAT and other standardized tests are based largely on vocabulary, and research has demonstrated that performance on vocabulary tests correlates positively with academic success. Other teachers place great emphasis on knowledge of grammar, usage, and diction on the assumption that mastery of the conventions of Standard English is the key to success in academics and in the business world. Still others expect demonstrations of wide-ranging knowledge of particular literature and of the terms and concepts of formal literary study. Of course, most teachers value much more than vocabulary, spelling, grammar, and literary terms—they value process. Whatever the criteria, we have given grades with confidence and even assumed that the grades given by teachers with very different criteria for performance in English were somehow comparable and indicated proficiency in the same field.

With the shift toward a discussion of common standards of performance for all students, many educators found confirmation for their own dissatisfaction with assessment systems based on the application of idiosyncratic criteria. They began to look at the use of common standards to judge performances of many types in the "real world." In real world performance, standards are based on the performance of professionals who exemplify the highest possible achievement in that field. Examples commonly come from sports such as baseball. Everyone who plays or follows baseball has internalized criteria for evaluating the performance of baseball players based on standards set by their favorites. The seven-year-old who plays Little League ball for the first time holds his bat, pitches the ball, and covers the bases in as close an approximation of Darryl Strawberry or Frank Viola as possible. The beginning figure skater strives for the grace of Kristi Yamaguchi, the athleticism of Midori Ito, and the elegance of Nancy Kerrigan.

Similar standards exist in the area of language performance, and whether educators are conscious of it or not, those standards are in mind when assessing performance. As the exercise above indicated, it is relatively easy to name the standard setters. It is considerably harder to delineate the standards. In Kazuo Ishiguro's book *The Remains of the Day* (1989), the narrator is a British butler named Stevens who reflects on a debate that went on through the years among the members of his profession on the question, What makes a great butler? There was, Stevens said, "no serious dispute as to the identity of the men who set the standards" among the butlers of his generation, but rather the question centered on "what precisely is this greatness? Just where or in what does it lie?" The same situation may exist among educators as we try to identify the standards for any of the areas of language use that we practice and teach. We may find some general agreement as to who the standard setters are (though we might have some very passionate debates over some nominees). We could probably agree generally on Shakespeare and a few other writers. We might concur on the public speaking ability of John F. Kennedy or Martin Luther King, Jr. But generalizing from the performance of individual standard setters to standards will not be easy. Nonetheless, it is essential that we make an attempt if we are to help our students to reach and surpass those standards.

I will examine each of the four general functions of language use that I have identified to determine what standards for performance exist for each of those functions of language.

Aesthetic Response and Expression

The category of aesthetic response and expression includes all uses of language commonly referred to as literary or artistic. As I am defining the category, aesthetic response and expression encompass reading and listening of the type Rosenblatt calls "aesthetic," and writing or speaking in the mode that Britton calls "poetic," as well as some of what he calls "expressive." These aesthetic uses of language all come under a general category of language use that Britton calls "language in the spectator role." Britton's own description of the roles of spectator and participant may be a helpful place to start in differentiating language functions:

> When we talk about our own affairs, clearly we can do so either as participant or as spectator. If I describe what has happened to me in order to get my hearer to do something for me, or even to change his opinion about me, then I remain a participant in my own affairs and invite him to become one. If, on the other hand, I merely want to interest him, so that he savours with me the joys and sorrows and surprises of my past experiences and appreciates with me the

intricate patterns of events, then not only do I invite him to be a spectator, but I am myself a spectator of my own experience.... I don't think it is far-fetched to think of myself talking not about my own past, but about my future, and again, doing so in either of the two roles. As participant I should be planning, and asking my listener to participate by helping or advising or just "giving me the necessary permission." As spectator I should be day-dreaming, and inviting my listener to share in that kind of pleasure. (Britton 1982, 49)

Britton's explanation of the spectator role starts with an analysis of informal spoken language—"the kind of gossip about events that most of us take part in daily"—but includes writing that is considered "literature." In a 1968 essay, "Response to Literature" (in Britton 1982), Britton defined literature "as a particular kind of utterance— an utterance that a writer has 'constructed' not for use but for his own satisfaction." Summing up his spectator role, he wrote, "When we speak this language, the nearest name I can give it is 'gossip'; when we write it, it is literature" (37).

The category I call aesthetic response and expression is language use that allows the individual to find and contemplate meaning, to reflect on life and experience, and to formulate one's own version of life or the world. When we read literature for pleasure or for the satisfaction of the experience or when we talk with other readers or viewers about the ways in which a book or film or play has moved us, we are using language for aesthetic purposes. When we express our views of the world through our own storytelling or by composing poems or song lyrics or writing plays, we are also engaged in aesthetic expression.

I want to start our consideration of language outcomes with this category of language for two main reasons. The first is because it is the most personal and, I think, the most humanizing use of language. Traditionally, the study of the humanities has involved reading the stories of the peoples of the world—the myths, legends, and fables by which groups of people made sense of their world. The sharing of stories between individuals and between cultures is ultimately a sharing of selves. That sharing continues to be essential to human development and to cross-cultural and interpersonal understanding in today's expanding global society.

The second reason for starting with this category is that aesthetic language use is often the most neglected in formal schooling as students move into upper grades. For some students, especially those in vocational or remedial programs, little attention is given to the reading of literature. In other programs in the school, a considerable amount of literature may be read, but in spite of the time devoted to literature, all too often the aesthetic stance of reading for the lived-through experience is ignored; literature is read to get something done—to pass a test or locate specific information. Little time in school is spent reading literature for the joy of the experience. Few conversations in school about literature or films or live performances sound like the conversations of adults who come together in book discussion groups or who discuss performances they have seen. Instead, talking and writing about literature in school is most likely to be in the transactional mode of writing or speech (Applebee 1978, 16), aimed at finding the correct understanding of the text.

If it is true that too little time and attention is given in school to language in the spectator role, one reason may be that the standards for performance of this type are considered highly personal and subjective. Teachers are reluctant to intervene in the development of this type of language and are even more reluctant to evaluate demonstrations of it.

We can identify distinguishing features of each function of language use that indicate assessment standards. For aesthetic response and expression, the most important distinguishing feature is precisely that it is *personal*. The connections the individual makes in aesthetic language are to life experiences and private associations.

Louise Rosenblatt describes the aesthetic stance toward reading as focusing the reader's attention not only on the public meanings of the words but also on the "associations, feelings, attitudes, and ideas that these words and their referents arouse within him" (1978, 25). In her theory, every individual has an experiential/linguistic reservoir from which to draw associations to make meaning in the reading of a text. Every transaction with a text involves a mix of public and private meanings, but in a predominantly aesthetic transaction the private aspects of sense are accorded a higher proportion of attention (Rosenblatt 1989, 161).

Classroom reading of literature seldom encourages aesthetic experience. Rosenblatt points out that the design of classroom activities and textbook questions often prevent students from taking an aesthetic stance toward a text. When the poem in a third-grade book is introduced by the question, "What facts does this poem teach you?" the student reads to extract information rather than to experience the imaginary world of the poem itself. Perhaps one reason aesthetic transactions are not regularly encouraged in classrooms is that teachers equate personal responses with emotional response and see little value for emotion as part of the academic study of literature. Rosenblatt, Iser, Bleich, and other Reader Response critics make it clear that literary or aesthetic experiences are not merely emotional, though they include emotional responses. By contrast, efferent transactions, which focus on gaining information, are not devoid of emotion. For example, newspaper accounts of the plight of the homeless or war victims often produce strong emotional responses in readers whose primary purpose in reading is to obtain information.

Aesthetic reading experiences are personal in that they involve not only emotional responses but also the images, ideas, interpretations, and judgments evoked by the text. The "poem" that is the object of transactional interpretation and analysis is not the text on the page but an evocation re-created in the transaction. The transaction is personal in that the poem, or re-created text, is different from the text re-created by any other reader or, in fact, from any other reading by the same reader—the same text can occasion a different "poem" when read by the same reader in another context. I particularly like Iser's explanation of the personal nature of literary experience.

> The impressions that arise . . . will vary from individual to individual, but only within the limits imposed by the written as opposed to the unwritten text. In the same way, two people gazing at the night sky may both be looking at the same collection of stars, but one will see the image of a plough, and the other will make out a dipper. The "stars" in a literary text are fixed; the lines that join them are variable. The author of the text may, of course, exert plenty of influence on the reader's imagination—he has the whole panoply of narrative techniques at his disposal—but no author worth his salt will ever attempt to set the *whole* picture before his reader's eyes. If he does, he will very quickly lose his reader, for it is only by activating the reader's imagination that the author can hope to involve him and so realize the intentions of his text. (Iser 1980, 57)

The personal nature of the "poem" that is the re-created text is an indication of the individual's level of active involvement in evoking a literary work of art. This involvement can be observed, encouraged, and assessed in the classroom. The extent to which the reader can make personal meaning in the transaction is one of the standards by which literature reading proficiency can be measured.

Iser's comments above on the process of reading literature point out another important consideration in identifying standards for reading of this type: the limits imposed by the text. In reading literature, even more than in reading for information, the reader must heed the particular words of the text.

> During the literary experience, concentration on the words of the text is perhaps even more keen than in an efferent reading. The reader must pay attention to all that these words, and no others, these words, moreover, in a particular sequence, summon up for him. When a fire breaks out, the man reading the directions for use of a fire extinguisher will pay no attention to whether the word is

"fire," "flame," or "combustion." But the aesthetic stance heightens awareness of the words as signs with particular visual and auditory characteristics *and* as symbols. What is lived through is felt constantly to be linked with the stimulus of the words. (Rosenblatt 1978, 29)

This is an important concept both in defining standards for assessing student proficiency in the reading of literature and especially in distinguishing aesthetic from efferent reading. Whereas in efferent reading the important consideration may be the individual's ability to remember and explain significant information and ideas extracted *from* the text, in aesthetic reading the individual contemplates responses to the very words, lines, images, and structures *of* the text. For this reason paraphrases, summaries, and abridgments can be said to deprive the student of a transaction with the literary text. The Cliffs Notes version of *Hamlet* is not Shakespeare's *Hamlet* and does not invite (or even allow) the reader to read from an aesthetic stance. Similarly, to be told that in "A narrow fellow in the grass" Emily Dickinson describes her fear of snakes is not the same as contemplating a personal response to the phrase "zero at the bone." Aesthetic readings require us to ask ourselves, Why these words? and, Why this way? Sophisticated readers are able to ask whether the emotion evoked by the text is valid or if the text is manipulative. They question whether the narrator is trustworthy, whether the plot is reasonable or contrived. And they do all those things by paying close attention to the words and structures of the text. The reader's awareness of how textual elements arouse particular responses constitutes a standard for literary reading that can be observed, encouraged, and assessed.

The standards for reading (or listening or viewing) from an aesthetic stance derive from attention to the two elements of the transaction: the reader and the text. As teachers we look for evidence of readings that are *personal* (drawn from the individual's private linguistic/experiential reservoir) and *textual* (clearly tied to the particular elements of this text).

When attention shifts from reading and listening for aesthetic response to writing and speaking for aesthetic response and expression, I suggest that we start with the same criteria for standards discussed above in terms of reading. Most educators value written and oral responses that are both personal and textual. Assessment of student aesthetic responses is based on the written and/or oral articulation of those responses. Often in classrooms the vehicle for the responses is classroom discussion, response logs, journals, or some other informal product. Unlike other classroom writing or speech, these responses are not evaluated for form or correctness but are an important element in observations of students' ability to read literature successfully. Writing in logs and journals is an example of what Britton calls expressive writing. Such writing is personal in the nature of the content and through its connections with the individual's past life and literary experiences, as well as in the nature of the language in which it is expressed.

The first audience for writing of this type is the writer, who writes in a journal to investigate personal responses by using the language that renders those responses most meaningfully or exactly. At some later time the student may take the entries from the journal and develop them into writing that is more public in nature, whether poetic or transactional, although the immediate purpose of expressive writing in a journal is to capture the response, not to explain it. It may be that personal expressive writing can be evaluated only by its presence and not its quality as this type of writing is so personal that it only has to satisfy the writer. When observing student ability to write for aesthetic response, educators should be much more concerned with the process than with the final product. Is the student able to write about personal responses to the text? Does the journal or log provide insights that later show up in more public writing and speaking about the text? Is the writing in the journal about the *text* and its features? Asking such questions helps instructors and students to focus on the aesthetic experience.

As soon as writing goes public—that is, as soon as it is intended for an audience other than the writer—standards of convention and form begin to matter. In writing for an external audience, one always relies on the audience recognition of shared conventions. Suzanne Langer says "the recognition of structure gives the mind its ability to find meanings" (1930, 132). Along those same lines, Robert Scholes asserts "reading is possible only to the extent that the actual reader shares a semantic and syntactic field with the writer" (1985, 48). Even the most personal writing intended for an audience must exhibit recognized standards of clarity, coherence, and style.

While these standards are required of writing in all modes, the meaning of each term varies somewhat by mode. For example, the standard for clarity in personal expressive or literary texts doesn't demand an absence of ambiguity. On the contrary, as Iser points out, "A literary text must be conceived in such a way that it will engage the reader's imagination in the task of working things out for himself, for reading is only a pleasure when it is active and creative" (1980, 51). The extent to which the text relies on the active participation of the reader to fill in the gaps varies immensely across the spectrum of literary texts, and there will be disagreement as to whether particular texts are too obscure or too straightforward to be good literature. For some readers Joyce's *Finnegans Wake* and Eliot's "The Wasteland" demand too much of the reader to be considered great literature; for others, some popular detective novels or docudramas are too transparent or fixed in meaning to be classified as literature. However, within this broad range of texts considered to be literary, one common element is an expectation that the text be both clear and accessible to the audience at the same time that it is richly polysemous. Thus, students' literary writing, expressive and poetic, must be clear and coherent enough to reward active engagement of a reader at the same time that it is ambiguous enough to allow imaginative re-creation by the reader.

In addition to clarity and ambiguity, personal expressive writing should feature a personal style that reveals the writer as a unique individual. By personal style I don't mean flowery and artificial expression or exotic vocabulary. Rather, style is the personal element in the writing that corresponds with the personal element in reading—the individual's imprint as unique and identifiable as a fingerprint, the element in the writing that calls out to the reader and provokes a response. Style reveals the writer behind the text and allows the reader to glimpse the writer's soul. Like the personal element in reading, style includes the emotional but goes beyond to include the writer's beliefs, principles, and biases. Peter Elbow states that writing of this type "renders" rather than explains, and one standard for assessing personal expressive writing and speech might be the extent to which it "renders" the personality of the writer or speaker effectively.

When attention is turned to writing and oral performance that is more properly poetic, all the standards used to assess the poetic writing of professional writers apply. Every genre has its own conventions, and standards and criteria for evaluating poetic products of all types are commonly available. But evaluating specific texts is not the same as assessing the habitual performance of an individual as a producer of poetic language—a "poet." To evaluate a text I believe most often readers consider the personal nature of the insights and the effectiveness with which those insights are communicated to an audience, the originality of vision and expression, and the connections with our own views and experiences.

Information and Understanding

If language for aesthetic response and expression is neglected in the school curriculum, language for information and understanding is in danger of overemphasis. Such is our respect for factual knowledge that often the most complex issues and even artistic experiences tend to be reduced to some version of Sergeant Friday's quest for "just the facts." There are many reasons for this concern with the acquisition of factual knowledge. One increasingly pressing reason is the comparison of American students with students from other developed nations where exit exams call for demonstration of knowledge of enormous quantities of factual information. The example of Japan is most frequently cited as American businessmen and politicians seek for reasons (or scapegoats) to explain the edge Japan has gained over the United States in international economic competition. Some critics of the American educational system have produced reports decrying the fact that American teenagers interviewed in shopping malls can't identify the capital city of Kansas or the continent on which Sri Lanka is located. Such reports may lead to the false conclusion that the acquisition of factual knowledge is not valued in our schools. In reality, the curriculum—and especially the testing—in our schools is too centered on factual information without comprehension. What is needed is a better system for helping students make productive use of information rather than more accurate parroting of decontextualized facts.

Another reason for the focus of attention on the acquisition of information is the mystique surrounding the possession of and ability to recall specific decontextualized facts. That mystique is demonstrated in the popular culture in the overwhelming popularity and durability of "Jeopardy," and Trivial Pursuit. In academic circles, the same views are reflected by the success of E.D. Hirsch's *Cultural Literacy*, with its companion *Dictionary of Cultural Literacy*, and the assorted volumes of *What Your First (Second, Third, Fourth, Fifth, Sixth) Grader Needs to Know*.

So ingrained in the American system is this respect for memorized lists of facts that often the tests by which major decisions are made about students (college admission, graduation, promotion, remediation) are tests of factual recall of specific information (spelling, vocabulary, grammar rules, names, dates). Such tests are called "objective" and carry with them an aura of scientific validity.

Merely memorizing isolated facts is useless. The crucial question is how to correlate the acquisition of knowledge with the ability to find and transmit information and understanding in a variety of contexts for real purposes. The standards implicit in demonstrations of knowledge of the Trivial Pursuit variety are not the standards of a process view of learning. However, in the process curriculum the ability to acquire and to transmit information is a value, and standards for using language effectively for that purpose can be described.

A first standard for using language for information and understanding distinguishes itself clearly from the aesthetic use of language. Whereas language for aesthetic response and expression is primarily personal, language for information and understanding is predominantly public. In Rosenblatt's explanation of the aesthetic-efferent continuum, the most purely efferent (or informational) reading events are those that rely almost exclusively on the public aspects of sense. In reading from this stance the individual has a greater need to consider the author's purpose and to reach consensus with other readers. Rosenblatt refers to the importance of differentiating the criteria of validity for efferent reading and for aesthetic reading: "In efferent reading, the student has to learn to focus attention mainly on the public, referential aspects of consciousness and to ignore private aspects that might distort or bias the desired publicly verifiable or justifiable interpretation" (1989, 163). Ignoring rather than focusing on the personal aspects of consciousness is essential to the reader's acquisition of information to use for some public purpose.

The same sense of purpose that guides the focus of attention for reading from an efferent stance is found in writing. When writers focus on public aspects of sense to write to "get something done," they purposely choose language and structures that are analytical and unambiguous in order to make the intended meaning as clear as possible. This type of writing is included in what Britton calls *transactional writing,* writing to accomplish some real work. Among the types of writing that fall into this mode are informational texts common to academic investigation and reporting. Other types include persuasive and analytical writing, which are discussed with critical analysis and evaluation.

A second standard for informational language is efficiency. If the purpose of language in this mode is to get things done, it follows that a measure of language effectiveness is how efficiently it accomplishes its purpose. Efficiency determines the organization of informational writing. The qualities of conciseness, precision, and the logical arrangement of details relate to the goal of presenting information in the most efficient and least distracting way. Particular standards of conciseness, precision, and logic vary across cultural groups and discourse communities but in informational language these qualities matter nonetheless.

A third standard for informational language use relates to validity or verifiability. While invention and imaginative connections are valued in aesthetic language, the major concern in informational language use is that it be accurate and well founded.

The counterbalance to the standard of validity and verifiability is the fifth standard of authority. If it is important that the writer supports a presentation of information through reference to outside testimony, then it is equally important that the writer establish a right to speak with authority. Bartholomae and Petrosky in *Facts, Artifacts, and Counterfacts* (1986) argue that the student writer "must assume an authority that, in a very real sense, she does not have. . . . as though [s]he were a member of the academy." In their view, authority is "achieved through an act of writing" rather than through a quality of vision that precedes the act. The course in basic reading and writing that Bartholomae and Petrosky describe began with a consideration of two features in student writing: "(1) the ways students textually established their authority as readers—their right to speak—and (2) the ways they located, then arranged and accounted for the points they were willing to call 'significant' in what they read" (19).

Some instructors may feel uncomfortable ascribing value to a standard that calls for posturing or playing at authority, but experience with performance in other areas reflect this same need to take on the desired role to gain membership in the group. Frank Smith uses a good metaphor when he calls on teachers to bring their students into the "literacy club" (1988). Like the other clubs that people join, the literacy club is composed of members who participate in and value the activities of the club: reading and writing. The club of academic writers is a particular branch of the literacy club with its own specialized discourse, characterized by a tone of authority meant "to exclude ordinary people" (Elbow 1991, 146). Informational writing, then, is assertive. It aims at getting something done by claiming the right of the writer to determine what is significant.

These qualities of informational reading and writing also underlie the standards for listening and speaking for information and understanding. Oral language in the transactional mode is expected to be public, efficient, valid and verifiable, and authoritative, although it may range in scope from giving directions to motorists to delivering formal presentations at professional conferences to clarifying points of law from the bench of the Supreme Court.

The ability to read, write, listen, and speak for information and understanding as it is defined by Rosenblatt, Britton, Elbow, Bartholomae, and Petrosky goes far beyond the recall and recitation of factual information that educational reformers seem to be calling for. Language used for information and understanding demands the ability to see relationships, focus attention selectively, and determine and explain significance—which are all necessary to make one's understanding clear to an audience and essential for academic study and professional discourse.

Critical Analysis and Evaluation

Critical analysis is not a discrete category of language. Rosenblatt discusses the category as a component of aesthetic as well as efferent reading, and Britton includes critical analysis and evaluation in the transactional mode. I consider the category separately here because the standards for assessing critical thinking, reading, writing, listening, and speaking are distinct from those of the other function categories I identified. In general we can define critical analysis and evaluation as the application of particular criteria in the formation of opinions and judgments about texts, experiences, and ideas. The essential factor in language use for critical analysis and evaluation is the ability to observe and analyze experiences from the perspective of particular sets of values or criteria. The values and criteria can come from many sources; each of us has a large and constantly expanding repertoire of criteria to use selectively. These criteria may be personal, cultural, or formal, and the individual may move in and out of the criteria of a number of codes in the evaluation of an experience.

For example, consider a group of adults emerging from a movie theater. They discuss the film they've seen, and their assessments of it are at first based solely on their personal tastes. The same group switches from their own personal criteria to more objective considerations of the technical aspects of film making, and the individual positions also shift somewhat as they comment on the cinematography, the acting, the sound track, the plot development, and so on.

When the focus of the discussion turns to cultural aspects of the film, yet another shift occurs. One person rejects the film's stereotyping of Italian Americans as mobsters, another finds the film's portrayal of women troubling, and someone else argues that the depiction of the American legal and judicial systems is inaccurate. Cultural criteria, of course, do not always result in negative analyses. One viewer praises the film for its excellence according to other cultural criteria—commending the film for its authenticity, its attention to detail, and strong sense of family.

This analysis of a film from a variety of criteria, some personal and some external, results in a widely expanded and multidimensional understanding of the film and of each individual's initial response to it. As the example indicates, a capable critic moves from highly personal criteria to a variety of more public criteria. One indicator of the proficiency of an individual as a critical thinker and language user is the ability to entertain and to articulate interpretations and analyses of a text from the criteria of a variety of cultural and critical perspectives and to "see and affirm the truth of contrary points of view" (Elbow 1986, 141).

Both Rosenblatt (1978) and Robert Scholes (1985) make the point that criticism is always made on behalf of a group. All individuals are members of particular cultures, subcultures, and social groups and, as members of those groups, they have internalized value and belief systems. The individual selects the perspective of a particular group to analyze and critique a text or experience. The process of selecting and applying criteria from a particular perspective is not always a conscious one. Often the criteria are so internalized, the individual is not even aware of the bases for judgments. A challenge for teachers is to help bring the process of selecting and applying criteria in critical analysis and evaluation to the conscious level.

Standards for critical analysis and evaluation relate to this selection and application of criteria. Because those criteria will come from a vast array of perspectives, they will vary from personal to social to formal. The standards relate to the selection, application, and articulation of appropriate criteria in evaluating a particular text or experience.

Another standard for critical analysis and evaluation is the recognition and accommodation of different evaluations of the same text or experience. Sophisticated critics recognize that varied and conflicting evaluations will result when different criteria are applied. In describing literary criticism, Rosenblatt argues that the critic "needs to recognize that varying valuations of the same work may result both from the application of different categories of criteria *and* from the differing hierarchies of values within any one category" (1978, 156). She gives an example from the category of formal literary criticism: Although both scope and structure are important elements in formal literary criticism, individual critics may value one of those elements more than the other. A critic who thinks structure is more important than scope may judge *Pride and Prejudice* to be superior to *War and Peace*. On the other hand, the critic who considers scope more important may prefer *War and Peace*.

A similar selection of criteria is used in analysis and evaluation of nonliterary experiences. Consider two political analysts evaluating the 1991 war in the Persian Gulf from a humanitarian perspective who disagree in their judgment of the war. One believes it to have been a success because a tyrant was prevented from imposing his rule on an unwilling nation, while the other analyst judges the war a failure because of the cost in human lives. A tolerance for ambiguity and an understanding that different judgments will result from the use of different criteria are indicators of sophisticated critical thinking.

Another standard for critical analysis and evaluation is the degree to which an analysis contextualizes the event by making clear to an audience the assumptions and values underlying the selection, formulation, and application of the criteria. An unsophisticated analysis or evaluation may not even demonstrate a conscious understanding of the nature and source of its criteria. Many times people present judgments or opinions as if they were absolute or based on universally held values without recognizing that these judgments are rooted in a particular perspective. People are often unable to articulate what criteria they are using, let alone the assumptions and values supporting those criteria. In the field of literary criticism, the call of Adrienne Rich and other critics to "revisit" traditional literary texts from a feminist perspective encouraged many readers to recognize that previous analyses of those works were made from a patriarchal perspective, a perspective that Judith Fetterley says includes misogyny as one of its characteristics. Yet to many male and female critics, those patriarchal elements were previously invisible. Contextualizing the analysis makes the underlying values and assumptions of a writer's or speaker's perspective explicit and allows us to recognize why we see and judge as we do.

Social Interaction

The category of language for social interaction is problematic in that some people argue that it is not a discrete function of language. Often, the argument is made that all language is social, and when socially interacting, people use language in a combination of the functions already described. Certainly there is some justice to this argument. When we meet at the coffee table at a break in a conference or at a cocktail party, we do indeed share information, pass on instructions for getting something done, or analyze recent political events. Such language experiences seem to fall quite neatly into the categories of informational and critical language use. We might even be involved in aesthetic language use, telling amusing stories or poignant anecdotes whose main purpose seems to be to move an audience. However, there is a fundamental difference in much of the social language we use: The primary function of language for social interaction is to build a relationship with another. Britton calls such language *expressive*, and although he acknowledges this language can be either written or spoken, it is more common to conversation. Expressive language is, the "language of all ordinary face-to-face speech" (1982, 97). The topic of conversation is usually chosen not to get something important done but to find a common bond to allow people to get to know one another better. Interrupted conversations, for example, are often not resumed since the speaker feels no compulsion to finish the discussion.

This social use of language may seem trivial compared to the functions of language considered previously, but the ability to form positive relations with others is an extremely important ability in today's world. The benefits of this ability for family and friends are obvious, but the social use of language is equally valuable for participation in public life. Much attention is given today to the skills needed for success in the workforce, and perhaps no skill is as beneficial as the ability to use language to build positive relationships. Diplomats, health- care workers, teachers, lawyers, insurance agents, and salespeople all rely on face-to-face interactions with other people and need to be skillful in language for social interaction.

Effective social language is close to the speaker and to the context (Britton 1982, 96). The speaker and the topic are equally revealed, and what the speaker chooses to reveal personally is determined to a great extent by the desired kind of relationship. For example, a successful counterworker at a fast food restaurant conveys to customers friendliness, efficiency, and a sensitivity to customer needs. Likewise, in the realm of international relations, harmonious relations among nations may depend as much on the small talk exchanged in the Rose Garden or at dinner as on the formal negotiations at the summit table. The common element in social interaction is the focus on the people involved in the immediate situation—language that tries to win sympathy, goodwill, and understanding. According to Britton, language used for social interaction is "the form of language by which most strongly we influence each other" (1982, 97).

In the previous examples I refer to spoken language use, but writing is of course also used for social interaction, and writing for this function shares the characteristics and standards associated with oral language. While letters written for school exercises may seem artificially formal, the letter writing that students do on their own—whether notes passed surreptitiously or letters mailed to vacationing friends—often reflect the tone, language, and even the cadence of normal conversation.

Standard English puts a distance between the speaker or writer and the text. To some extent Standard English depersonalizes the text in order to make it more public. Aesthetic writing may be highly personal, but at the same time it is particularly concerned with form and artistic expression. Only in language used for social interaction does the standard require that the language be as close to the conversational language of the individual as possible while conveying the message appropriately to the audience. In writing for social inter-action, the most important element being conveyed is the self.

Reading for social interaction involves a similar focus on build-ing a relationship with another, either the author of the piece or a person with whom the reader is sharing the reading experience. We read and reread letters and notes from absent friends in order to feel their presence. We exchange journals and diaries as a way of getting to know another. Sometimes we read favorite pieces aloud with someone as a way of being together.

There is a sense in which all reading is social. Alan Purves has said that it always takes two to read a text. At the very least reading involves a transaction between two meaning makers, the writer and the reader—even when the writer is the self of an earlier time. In many cases a community of readers is involved in reading together and expanding individual understanding through shared responses. But, as the examples above suggest, not all those instances constitute reading for social interaction as I have defined it here. As long as the text and its meaning are the primary focus of the reading, the reading belongs more properly to either the aesthetic, informational, or critical category. It is only when the focus is on being with another that the reading belongs to the category of social interaction.

Summary

In trying to discover internalized standards of language use, it is useful to start with language functions recognizably distinct to try to discover what distinguishes those functions. I have identified four common functions of language: aesthetic, informational, critical, and social.

Aesthetic

- *Meaning:* The individual will read and listen to enjoy and appreciate texts, to personally relate texts, and to respond sensitively to texts with diverse social, historical, and cul-tural dimensions. As a writer and speaker, the individual will use written and oral language for self-expression and entertainment.
- *Focus:* On the person; the unique connections and meaning that the individual makes in the "lived-through experience."
- *Distinguishing Features:* Personal and textual.

Informational

- *Meaning:* As a reader and listener, the individual will collect data, facts, or ideas; discover relationships, concepts or generalizations; and use knowledge acquired from texts or oral presentations. As a writer and speaker, the individual will use oral and written language to acquire, interpret, apply, and transmit information in appropriate forms.
- *Focus:* On the message; the use of the information to accomplish a public purpose.
- *Distinguishing Features:* Public, efficient, valid and verifiable, and authoritative.

Critical

- *Meaning:* As a reader and listener, the individual will use personal and external criteria from multiple perspectives to form opinions or to make judgments about ideas and information in written texts and oral presentations. As a writer and speaker, the individual will use personal and external criteria from multiple perspectives to express opinions and judgments about issues, ideas, and experiences.
- *Focus:* On the perspectives; the recognition of the assumptions and values that underlie opinions and judgments.
- *Distinguishing Features:* Cultural (that is, derived from a particular group), flexible, and contextualized.

Social

- *Meaning:* As a reader, writer, listener, and speaker, the individual will use oral and written language to establish and maintain positive interpersonal relationships.
- *Focus:* On the relationship; the establishment of trust and harmony among individuals and groups.
- *Distinguishing Features:* Interpersonal, immediate, and natural.

Chapter Two

Characteristics of Performance

What do we as educators look for when assessing students' language proficiencies? We can look for those features of meaning making essential to the function as they allow us to distinguish between the student's ability to read critically or for information. What characteristics, then, allow us to distinguish a beginning reader from a more proficient reader? There are factors that indicate increasing proficiency in many kinds of performance, and when discussing artists, athletes, musicians, craftsmen, actors, cooks, scientists, or politicians, we commonly refer to these factors. I call these factors *characteristics of performance*, which include range, flexibility, connections, conventions, and independence. In assessing the language proficiencies of an individual, I suggest that we consider each of those characteristics for each of the outcomes. I think it is useful to consider these characteristics to the fullest extent possible as they apply to the functions, although it is important to avoid making distinctions among the language domains of reading, writing, listening, and speaking. The differences among the domains are significant, but they are also misleading if they prevent our recognizing that the making of meaning is, as Ann Berthoff has consistently emphasized, the common activity of all language use. What do each of the characteristics allow us to see and say about a student's language?

Range

The concept of range includes the dimensions of breadth and depth. In describing language ability in general, range applies to a number of elements over which the individual can demonstrate control: subjects, topics, themes, registers, modes, genres, patterns of usage, levels of diction, grammatical forms, rhetorical forms, stylistics, discourse, and conventions. The particular relevant topics that apply vary according to the particular outcome under consideration. For example, the range of genres might be important in discussing reading for aesthetic response, but the range of patterns of usage might be more important in discussing informational writing.

The depth of range refers to the complexity and sophistication of language and thinking. The nature of the text and the expertise required of the intended audience are indicators of relative complexity. Professional journals, highly specialized technical manuals, expressionistic literature, academic treatises, and doctoral theses are typically beyond the general reader or writer and are meant for the expert or specialist.

The relation of breadth to depth when determining an individual's level of proficiency is not a simple matter. In many professions, individuals are generally recognized for the depth of their comprehension of and contributions to the scholarship of their discipline. The breadth of that understanding may be very narrow; often the most highly regarded experts in a field have an extremely narrow area of specialization. A biologist who writes a definitive treatise on the life cycle of the tsetse fly may have only general knowledge of reptiles, for instance, with a superficial understanding of ideas from other disciplines. Literary scholars who can explicate every line of Milton may know little of the writing of later poets. Narrow specialization is often regarded as an indication of expertise.

In the case of developing learners, however, most educators prefer wide-ranging exploration with some depth in chosen areas. Peter Elbow in *Embracing Contraries* defines "real learning" as "the ability to apply already-learned concepts to the widest range of data" combined with the "ability to construct new concepts" (1986, 12). The ability to experience learning as Elbow describes it requires that the student be provided with diverse opportunities for making meaning. Those experiences and the elements included in the range will vary for each of the language outcomes discussed below, but the goal of education is to provide experiences over a broad range with some depth.

Range in Aesthetic Response and Expression

A fundamental indicator of the individual's range in reading and responding to literature is the ability to read from different stances. The first issue to consider when determining an individual's range is to discover if reading occurs for "the lived-through experience" and at other times purposely takes a different stance to the text in order to find particular information in it. Does this individual, even in the reading of fiction and poetry, seem to focus on the accumulation of information? It may seem that reading from an aesthetic stance is natural or instinctive. But, as Rosenblatt points out, "perhaps because this distinction has tended to be taken for granted and has not been made explicit, many never learn to read aesthetically" (1978, 40). Therefore, in describing the range of the individual, I suggest that educators first determine whether there is evidence of aesthetic experiences or whether literature is read from an efferent stance.

Another essential aspect of range is the ability to read a variety of genres. The accomplished reader can read with authority in all genres and can articulate a response appropriate to the particular conventions of the genre. A response to a given poem will indicate not only that the accomplished reader is able to make connections between the poem and personal experience (an essential element in aesthetic response) but also between this poem, other poems of its type, and the body of poetry as a whole (Frye 1957, 96). The concept of genre is itself an essential understanding for the reader of literature. Recognizing what distinguishes one genre from another and what conventions to expect from each genre is often crucial to aesthetic response and expression.

A third essential indicator of aesthetic range is the variety of subject matter the individual reads, writes, and talks about in terms of topics, disciplines, and themes. Every teacher can describe students whose reading is limited to particular areas of individual interest. Whether this limited preference reflects a social or personal interest (fishing, sports, romances) or an academic focus (physics, history, political science), a narrow focus is considered undesirable. Most educators want developing minds to grapple with numerous topics and ideas, and they usually look for evidence of complexity and sophistication in the treatments of these topics. The student who reads *Zen and the Art of Motorcycle Maintenance* and responds to the many layers of meaning found there may be considered a more accomplished reader than the one who reads *Rumble Fish*, even though both books were chosen because of the reader's interest in motorcycles.

Other indicators of range in aesthetic response and expression are also important. Today many educators strive to develop in their students an appreciation of the literature of diverse cultures. The ability to read critically in multicultural literature—to recognize the commonalities while respecting the differences, to view life from the perspective of another set of cultural values—is a mark of sophistication.

Range in Informational Language

When using language to acquire and transmit information, individuals are constantly expanding their range of topics, issues, and disciplines. It may seem that anyone is capable of acquiring information on any topic or from any discipline, but teachers recognize the importance of prior knowledge for understanding new information. Schema theory explains that the process of acquiring information is based on existing knowledge in order to generate an understanding or interpretation of a text. Since prior knowledge of a text will vary considerably among students, meanings will vary, too. Any reader may find himself confronted with texts that the reader is unable to understand sufficiently. The sports page or the reviews of the latest rock albums may be as incomprehensible to the mature academic as a text of psychology or philosophy is to most adolescents. As previously noted, the wider the range of topics a student can understand and discuss, the higher our estimation of his literacy. But as educators we can't pretend that all knowledge is valued equally. While members of our society may consider it a mark of refined taste for an academic to have little knowledge of the popular culture, they tend to regard any gaps in students' knowledge, especially in areas of traditional academic study, as deficiencies.

A real understanding of any discipline includes knowledge not only of specific information related to topics and subject matter but also of how members of that discipline write and speak to each other. Is the content of some student textbooks really useful in bringing students into meaningful discussions of that discipline? Students who have read biology only in high school textbooks may be unable to understand the writing or lectures of real biologists, even though they have "studied" the topic being addressed. The issue of "authentic" material, a major concern to literature teachers, has implications for the investigation of issues in the content areas as well. I think it is valid to argue that unless the range of students includes primary source material in a discipline and the ability to use the discourse conventions of that discipline in writing and speaking, student authority over that discipline remains limited and understanding superficial. Whether focusing instruction on disciplinary conventions is a good thing needs to be explored. The value of privileged discourse communities that have limited access is questionable—educators may need to argue for more inclusive language in discussion across disciplines. For now, however, instructors need also to realize that the literacy club Frank Smith describes (1988) has many component groups, each with its own "set of social and authority relations" (Elbow 1991, 146) meant to exclude the uninitiated.

Range in Critical Language

An individual's critical range is related to the personal informational range, since the more schemata or "codes" an individual has in a reservoir of prior knowledge, the more diverse and complex an analysis and evaluation of a text or experience can be. Critical analysis requires, as discussed above, the ability to view an event from the perspective of a particular group and to critique the text or event based on the assumptions and values of that perspective. Adopting other perspectives is no simple matter since there are many possible perspectives within a given group and many different value priorities within those perspectives. The reader viewing a work from a feminist perspective, for example, has to decide which feminist perspective to favor and which of the values of that perspective are most important. The ability to make such decisions rests on the critic's understanding that there are many competing feminist perspectives, each with its own assumptions and value systems. Such a sophisticated reading of the world is a high expectation even for experienced adults, but it is, as Robert Scholes points out, "especially hard for students, whose own thoughts and values are likely to be constantly wavering and far from clear" (1985, 55).

Scholes and others refer to sets of assumptions and values as codes. Identifying two general categories of codes may be helpful in describing the range instructors expect of students. Though these categories are not really discrete, they nonetheless make useful distinctions. The first category I call critical, which refers to formal theoretical perspectives. The second category I call cultural, which refers to perspectives of groups identified by common language, geography, political structure, religion, or other such feature.

Even in a simpler time when the only critical perspective considered appropriate to classroom analysis of literature was New Criticism and the goal was to arrive at the correct interpretation and assessment of the work, the range of criteria was formidable since each genre and form have their own "grammar." Today's recognition of the inevitability and value of multiple perspectives makes the challenge much greater for teaching. Whether the classroom experience involves students in reading a text from several different perspectives or in analyzing the text from one agreed upon set of criteria, it is equally important students see *all* meanings as situated or contextualized, not just those that can be labeled as representing a "special interest group." In his report of the English Coalition Conference, Peter Elbow (1990) refers to the agreement among teacher participants on the value of helping students take a conscious theoretical stance.

> Thus the dominant theme of the conference came to be that what are seen as "normal" or "assumed" or "obviously true" views or practices—even "always already" principles—must be recognized to be just as much "special interest" as the views or practices commonly labeled as special interest. Groups in power tend to label smaller groups as special interest, not seeing that they themselves are special interest. . . . Nothing must be taken as normal, neutral, disinterested, inevitable, necessary, objective. People get to take charge of their reading and writing processes and not to be told what's right by virtue of authority. (Elbow 1990, 79)

Essential to the ability to take a critical stance is knowledge of a range of critical perspectives and an understanding of the underlying assumptions and values of those perspectives. The individual's facility in moving in and out of those perspectives is included in the discussion of flexibility, but I have assumed that critical flexibility depends on the possession of a substantial range of critical perspectives.

Range in Social Language

One increasingly important language-use demand is the ability to adapt one's language for a wide variety of social groups and situations. When teachers refer to the need to expand or develop their students' language, they commonly are concerned with the ability to use Standard English as a requirement for participation in the business and social life of the community—a position reflecting a general awareness that Standard English is used in all the functions language serves in the society, which gives it a high status. This status comes from the usefulness of English in the society rather than from some inherent quality of English as opposed to other languages represented in the American culture (Spanish, French Creole, Black English). The status of Standard English is not true for English in every society. Halliday describes a culture in which English is the "mother tongue of the inhabitants" but not a developed language. His example is worth looking at.

> In the Caribbean island of Sint Maarten, the mother tongue of the inhabitants is English. Education and administration, however, take place in Dutch; English is not normally used in these contexts. In Sint Maarten, English is an undeveloped language. The islanders find it hard to conceive of serious intellectual and administrative processes taking place in English. They are, of course, perfectly well aware that English is used in all these functions in Britain, the USA, and elsewhere. But they cannot accept that the homely English that they themselves speak (although dialectically it is of a quite "standard" type that is readily understood by speakers from outside) is the same language as English in its national or international guise. (Halliday 1978, 194)

Because English is the developed language of American society, American students need to develop their control of English in order to participate in all the areas of the society in which English is used. In Halliday's view, the process of developing a language consists of developing new *registers:* "A register is a set of meanings that is appropriate to a particular function of language, together with the words and structures which express these meanings" (1978, 195). The greater the range of registers, the more access an individual has to the aspects of the society that rely on those registers.

Helping students develop a range of registers is an essential step in helping them gain full access to their society, but language registers are not learned through formal instruction. Rather, it seems that they are acquired by trying them out in conversation with those around us. Halliday, in describing the way children acquire new registers, says:

> What matters most to a child is how much talking goes on around him, and how much he is allowed and encouraged to join in. There is strong evidence that the more adults talk to a child and listen to him and answer his questions, the more quickly and effectively he is able to learn. (Halliday 1978, 201)

Britton makes a similar point in describing the process by which learners use expressive language to learn to write and speak in all the transactional and poetic forms they need. He suggests a developmental hypothesis according to which expressive language "should be regarded as a matrix from which the other two categories would develop" (1982, 124). He also describes the value of expressive language.

> Our experience of chatting with people we know well in a relaxed and loosely structured way is thus a major resource we draw upon when we write expressively. And whether we write or speak, expressive language is associated with a relationship of mutual confidence, trust, and is therefore a form of discourse that encourages us to *take risks*, to try out ideas [or language forms] we are not sure of, in a way we would not dare to do in, say, making a public speech. In other words, expressive language (as a kind of bonus) is a form that favors exploration, discovery, learning. (Britton 1982, 124)

I am trying to make two points here about the range of language for social interaction. First, in order for a given person's range of social interaction to be as broad as possible, an individual will need the registers of language used in all those social situations. Second, those registers will be acquired through the context-bound speech of personal conversation between intimates that allows the learner to "try on" the concepts and structures of the new register in situations relatively free of fear of errors. Trying on a new register in this way is a very different process from the one sometimes seen in classrooms in which learners are encouraged to play at "writing like scientists" or "speaking like politicians," a teaching strategy that seems to rest on a belief that individuals acquire registers by imitating superficial conventions rather than by exploring new concepts and meanings and, in the process, acquiring mastery of the full register.

Flexibility

Range is an indicator of the scope of content of the individual's language performance; it identifies *what* the individual can read, write, understand, or say. Flexibility, on the other hand, refers to *how* the individual reads, writes, listens, and speaks, and I think flexibility is the most useful characteristic for distinguishing outcomes from behavioral objectives. Whereas behavioral objectives attempt to describe performance in certain prescribed conditions, outcomes assessment attempts to describe performance in varied and changing conditions. Flexibility—the ability to adjust one's performance to the demands of the immediate context—is an important indicator of the language user's sophistication.

Flexibility in Aesthetic Response and Expression

Louise Rosenblatt's (1978) transactional theory emphasizes the importance of context to the re-creation of the literary work. When a reader transacts with a familiar text in a new context, a different "poem" is recreated. Rosenblatt explains this process by reference to William James' concept of *selective attention:*

> The concept of selective attention is central to my definition of the aesthetic experience. It is helpful also in eliminating the notion of a necessarily conscious choice. The selective process operates in weighting responses to the multiple possibilities offered by the text and thus sets the degrees of awareness accorded to the referential import and to the experiential process being lived through. (Rosenblatt 1978, 43)

Teachers make use of the selective process when they purposely structure the classroom context to direct students' attention to particular aspects of a text. Thus, teachers sequence literary experiences so that similar themes and variations will be observed, diverse cultural perspectives on the same topic will be evident, the obvious presentation of an archetypal pattern in one work will make the same pattern perceptible in a subsequent work, one character will be a foil for another, and so on. The student who recognizes the expectations of the classroom context for reading the text will be more successful in focusing attention on its appropriate aspects to fit the frame of reference the teacher has provided. When instructors ask students to revisit a familiar work and to respond to it from the perspective of another text or to read a piece of literature particularly for its relevance to an immediate social situation, they test student flexibility. Students learn to change the focus of their attention as they transact with the text in particular contexts. Written and oral responses to the same text at different times and in different contexts indicate the flexibility of students for putting aside previous readings.

Flexibility in responding to aesthetic experiences is evident in the ability of individuals to fit language, style, form, and message to the intended audience, topic, purpose, and context. Individual responses can be made in any mode: expressive, poetic, or transactional. Responses may be in the highly personal language of journals and reading logs that may ignore the conventions of standard usage; they may employ the highly charged language of poetic expression whose sounds, shapes, and rhythms are as significant as the responses' meanings; they often will use the analytic language of the critical essay or research paper whose clarity and logic are meant to convince readers of the author's right thinking. When the form, mode, language, and style of the individual's responses in a great number of aesthetic experiences consistently seem right for the purpose, audience, and context, instructors can conclude the individual demonstrates exceptional flexibility.

Flexibility in Informational Language

We referred earlier to the range of registers an individual must have for full participation in all areas of the society. The ability to move in and out of those registers is an indication of an individual's flexibility in using language for information. As discussed with the concept of range, each discipline and area of human endeavor has its own registers. Nowhere is the great number of registers more apparent than in schools, where students moving from one classroom to another shift into the register of earth science for a forty-five minute instructional period and then into the register of literature for the next forty-five minutes. The ease with which a student does this shifting and the degree to which each register seems to be developed for an individual constitute the flexibility that distinguishes the sophisticated language user.

The relationships among registers within a language are complex, as Halliday (1978) makes clear in his discussion of the connections between the language of modern mathematics and the ordinary language of everyday use.

> In English, at least, modern mathematics has tended to redefine simple words rather than coining new ones for its technical terms. This in fact is part of the difficulty; the fact that a concept such as "set" has a precise mathematical definition may be obscured by the simplicity of the word itself.
>
> Be that as it may, "modern" mathematics does make greater demands on language than "traditional," partly because it is relatively nonnumerical, but perhaps even more because its relations with other aspects of life are emphasized more explicitly, whereas in earlier days, mathematics tended to remain quite separate from the rest of a child's experience.
>
> However, it would be a mistake to suppose that the language of mathematics (by which is meant the mathematical register, that form of natural language used in mathematics, rather than mathematical symbolism) is entirely impersonal, formal, and exact. On the contrary, it has a great deal of metaphor and even poetry in it, and it is precisely here that the difficulties often reside. Expressions such as "four from six leaves two" represent essentially concrete modes of meaning that take on a metaphorical guise when used to express abstract, formal relations (i.e., when interpreted as "$6-4 = 2$"). (Halliday 1978, 201–2)

Few language users, no matter how accomplished, are consciously aware of the distinctions between registers or the particular characteristics of those registers, yet hundreds of times a day many people switch automatically into the contextually appropriate register.

Another aspect of flexibility in using language for information is the individual's ability to adapt the mode of delivery to the specific context. In the language experiences Britton calls context bound, the speaker constantly watches for signals from the audience and shifts the examples, amount of elaboration, and emphasis according to the verbal and nonverbal responses of the audience. Good teachers, for example, are experts at watching their students during direct instruction for signs of recognition, confusion, drifting attention, or disagreement. They can hear the underlying questions and mis-apprehensions within students' verbal responses and can present the same information in other ways to address those confusions. They try to develop the same flexibility in their students by raising questions during students' presentations in the classrooms to force students to elaborate, define, or support their original statements.

Even in language situations meant to be relatively context-free, such as formal public speeches or writing for generalized audiences, flexibility is often called for. A public speaker may have to change a prepared text on the spot for any number of reasons: when the audience is different from what was expected, or the previous speaker used prepared material, or the overhead projector or teleprompter malfunctions. One who can make those changes without giving any indication of the changes has demonstrated control not only over the subject matter but also over presentational strategies. Similarly, the professional who can write with authority on the most esoteric issues of a particular discipline and can also make obscure or highly technical material accessible to a general audience demonstrates a degree of flexibility that distinguishes him from his peers.

Flexibility in Critical Analysis and Evaluation

As seen in the discussion of the range of critical perspectives within an individual's repertoire, an important mark of proficiency is the ability to analyze a text or event from multiple perspectives and to tolerate the ambiguity arising from evaluating the same event differently from each of those perspectives. The ease with which a person selects and applies appropriate and effective criteria from a variety of perspectives to produce convincing and powerful analyses and evaluations is indicative of that person's level of critical flexibility.

Like many features of effective language use, critical flexibility may appear to be virtually automatic in a sophisticated critic, or the process of selective attention to particular aspects of the text may occur almost automatically so that only on reflection will the individual be able to explain why those particular aspects seemed significant. For the student critic, the tendency will be to "articulate judgments in categories closely linked to their own life concerns" (Rosenblatt 1978, 157). As students gain experience and confidence as critics, they will apply criteria from a broad range of literary, cultural, ethical, and/or psychological perspectives. Ease in deciding which perspective to use or when a full understanding requires considering several perspectives is a mark of increasing critical maturity.

Connections

Perhaps the most important factor in assessing an individual's language competence is the ability to make connections, since all meaning making rests on linking what is newly encountered and what was previously known. Clearly the ability to make connections is related to an individual's range of knowledge and experience, but even individuals with vast experience and knowledge can differ in this ability.

The two aspects of real learning described by Peter Elbow (1986) are components of what I call an ability to make connections. The first, "the ability to apply already learned concepts to the widest range of data," relies, as Elbow explains it, on the interpenetration of formally and experientially learned concepts, what Vygotsky (1962) called "scientific concepts" and "spontaneous concepts" (Elbow 1986, 18). In Vygotsky's view the interpenetration of these two concept types allows the individual to recognize formally learned (scientific) concepts in real situations and to explain experientially learned (spontaneous) concepts in formal language. English teachers seek evidence of this interpenetration in the literary responses of their students: an ability to recognize instances of the concepts they have acquired from their formal study (literary concepts such as irony, tragedy, foreshadowing, or allegory), concepts they have acquired through experience (family loyalty, loneliness, or grief), or a combination of the two. Similar evidence can be seen in students' nonliterary reading and in their investigation of topics of interest across the disciplines.

The second of the aspects of real learning, the ability to invent new concepts or to think with metaphors, is also easy to observe in the student's articulation of a literary response or interpretation. Wolfgang Iser describes the reading process as one that requires the creative participation of the reader.

> Even in the simplest story there is bound to be some kind of blockage, if only because no tale can ever be told in its entirety. Indeed,

it is only through inevitable omissions that a story gains its dynamism. Thus whenever the flow is interrupted and we are led off in unexpected directions, the opportunity is given to us to bring into play our own faculty for establishing connections—for filling the gaps left by the text itself. (Iser 1980, 55)

Sometimes the gaps will be filled in by the reader through the application of a known concept as described in the section above, but at other times the literary response is more creative, relying on the reader's ability to think with metaphors. In an earlier section (pp. 8 and 9), I looked at Iser's discussion (1980) of the author's reliance on the reader's imagination in "realizing the intention of his text." Even though readers may be focusing on the same literary text, the images they find vary from one reader to another and depend on the individual connections each reader makes—where one sees a plough, another sees a dipper. The metaphors they find to make meaning in the texts of other writers expand the understanding of the text as well as the readers.

Readings of texts are as individual as the texts themselves, and particularly effective readings of literary works are often those that make conscious use of metaphor to resymbolize the text. I don't mean that those literary responses are themselves poetic discourse (although they might be), but that even responses written in the expressive or transactional modes often make conscious use of metaphors to express insights.

The ability to make connections through the application of already learned concepts and through thinking in metaphors manifests itself in many ways. John Mayher (1990) discusses the importance of "intertextuality," calling it "one of the key ingredients in developing the capacity to make more mature and sophisticated transactions." In Mayher's view, "We are always in the process of becoming good readers since every new text can at least potentially enrich and extend our competence as readers" (216). Mayher also analyzes the ability to make connections and its reliance on intertextuality.

> Clearly, the sophistication of response can and should be deepening throughout the school years. This depends on a variety of factors including each learner's growing experience of the world—hence the more connections which can potentially be made to the people and events one is reading about—and the growing repertoire of other texts which have been read which, themselves, enable connections to be made. . . . One does not have to be a deconstructionist to recognize that through reading (and being read to), readers have internalized a repertoire of textual conventions and genres, as well as characters and plots, and that this kind of cultural literacy plays a role in our transactions with all texts. (Mayher 1990, 220)

Similarly, Robert Scholes explains the necessity of making connections in the process of reading, interpreting, and criticizing literature as a matter of recovering essential codes.

> Reading is possible only to the extent that the actual reader shares a semantic and syntactic field with the writer. A "field" in this sense is a set of codes and paradigms that enable and constrain meaning. The further estranged the reader is from the writer (by time, space, language, or temperament) the more interpretation must be called upon to provide a conscious construction of unavailable or faded codes and paradigms. If we are going to read John Donne, for example, we must recover something of the codes of alchemy, Neoplatonism, Petrarchan erotics, early Anglican theology, and a feeling for the syntax and semantics of a spoken and written English vastly different from our own. (Scholes 1985, 48)

Scholes' theory of textuality may seem far removed from the daily concerns of high school English teachers, and yet every teacher has experienced the frustration of trying to teach literature of remote cultural contexts to students who have no connections with the historical traditions of those cultures. A great deal of class time is spent with the teacher explaining unfamiliar terms and references to the students in order to make a text accessible to them. The students who have experienced the process of recovering faded codes with a teacher will display over a number of years responses to literature containing an awareness of the tension between familiar codes and those of an author removed in time or place, so that students will demonstrate an ability to recover for themselves the codes necessary for a satisfying reading of the work.

Rosenblatt explains the process by which a reader develops a framework for negotiating the interplay between the codes of the author and reader as one that relies on both memory and curiosity as the reader moves almost automatically "through a continuing flow of responses, syntheses, readjustment, and assimilation" (1978, 58). Some readers will find frameworks that yield rich readings of the work and take into account all the aspects of the text in its the re-creation, but others will be less able to assimilate all the details of the text because of limitations in their previous experience of the language or referents of the text and will produce readings that are naive, superficial, or even invalid. Bartholomae and Petrosky (1986) have pointed out that any reading is a reduction of a text, but teachers are aware that not all readings are equal and that they need some criteria for distinguishing the quality of readings in the absence of an ideal or correct reading. Rosenblatt suggests the criterion of "the fullness and intensity of the reader's sense of his evocation, testing it not only by the fidelity to cues offered by the text but also by the complexity of the strands of awareness woven into a coherent structure" (1978, 154). Rosenblatt's criterion adds to the idea of the reader's ability to make connections (to "cues offered by the text") the notion of the appropriateness and efficacy of those connections (to produce "a coherent structure").

The work of Iser, Scholes, and Rosenblatt deals primarily with the importance of making connections in the process of responding to literature, but it is easy to see that the same process applies to making meaning from texts of any type: oral, visual, or written; literary or nonliterary. Similarly, it is the articulation of those connections in oral or written language that communicates the meaning to an audience and gives evidence of the complexity and originality of the thinking. Creative, metaphoric thinking calls attention to itself and causes the audience to see the concept or idea in a new way.

In arguing that the ability to make connections is the single most important factor in distinguishing skillful and successful learners and thinkers, I am suggesting that making connections is at the heart of making meaning for oneself as opposed to parroting the thinking of another. We all know people whose imaginative, insightful connections dazzle with their brilliance and show us facets of a familiar concept we had never seen. Some of those original thinkers are students, and the role of teachers is to encourage the playful and adventurous linking of ideas that will occasionally lead to genuine insight. For other students, teachers have to nurture and model the process of making connections. For those students even the most obvious connections are elusive, and the teacher's role is to supply some connections and remind the student of the value of creating connections with something familiar but apparently unrelated in order to make sense of new data.

Conventions

As the previous section indicates, the concept of conventions is integral to the ability to make connections. In their discussions of connections, Mayher, Scholes, Rosenblatt, and Elbow all refer to the repertoire of conventions the individual possesses. Student control of a wide range of conventions is readily recognized by teachers as essential to academic study as well as to full functioning in all areas of society. However, all too often discussion of conventions with reference to students' academic work is limited to the narrow range of surface-level conventions such as grammar, usage, diction, punctuation, spelling, and so on. But in assessing the individual's habitual performance as a language user, a much broader view of conventions is necessary to describe fully all the individual is able to do. This expanded view includes all the rhetorical and pragmatic conventions necessary for reading, writing, speaking, and listening for all of the various functions.

To assess student achievement of language outcomes, consider three general categories of conventions: literary conventions essential to poetic expression and reception, discourse conventions appropriate to the full range of writing and oral performance, and the surface-level mechanical conventions of particular concern in elementary and secondary education.

Northrop Frye in *Anatomy of Criticism* (1957) describes in detail the importance of conventions to literary criticism and production. "The problem of convention," Frye says, "is the problem of how art can be communicable, for literature is clearly as much a technique of communication as assertive verbal structures are" (99). Conventions in Frye's view include all those "expected associations" the poet uses to "communicate more rapidly." All poetic writing, according to Frye, falls somewhere on a continuum between "pure convention," in which a writer uses a traditional image or formal device merely because it has been used previously in the same way, to "anticonventional" or experimental writing that purposely tries to "break with convention." Regardless of where the work falls on the continuum, an understanding of the conventions that are being followed or violated is essential for a satisfying experience of the text. Among the conventions referred to by Frye are conventions of imagery, characterization, plot, and form.

One implication of Frye's recognition of the importance of conventions is the value of "highly conventionalized literature" for classroom study. Many teachers have discovered for themselves the usefulness of fairy tales, folk tales, popular music, and films for introducing their students to traditional patterns and images. Students who first discover conventional patterns in more easily accessible literature gradually become able to apply those patterns in reading and interpreting more obviously complex and demanding works. Student written and oral responses to newly encountered literary works and dramatic productions indicate that their understanding of those traditional patterns gives them a language for exploring the meaning of other works. Also, as students become familiar with the traditional patterns and images, they will begin to use those conventions in the production of literary pieces of their own, sometimes in a straightforward manner by writing their own fables or fairy stories, and at other times more subtly and creatively in parodies or modern realistic fiction.

Just as there are conventions particular to poetic writing, there are also conventions for transactional writing of all types for the areas of interaction within society. One important ability for students, especially for those who will continue their education at the university level, is the ability to use the conventions of academic discourse to produce those forms of transactional writing commonly expected in college classes. We shouldn't underestimate the complexity of this expectation. Language appropriate for academic investigation is very far removed from the vernacular of many students. Shirley Brice Heath's studies (1983) have shown the advantages students have when the language of the home approximates the language valued in the school. Bartholomae and Petrosky in *Facts, Artifacts, and Counterfacts* (1986) point out that students who are less successful in formal academic study often lack the authority over academic discourse more successful students exhibit. The problem is compounded since there is not just one discourse required of students in their academic study; each discipline has its own discourse and distinct conventions. Alan Purves points out that in the course of a day or week "students must be apprenticed to five or six rhetorical communities" (1988).

In an article in *College English*, Peter Elbow (1991) discusses the need for students to learn the conventions of academic discourse, the difficulty of determining what characterizes that discourse, and the tension between helping students learn those conventions and presenting what is really valuable in writing instruction. The conventions of academic discourse are in Elbow's view problematic. He maintains that what distinguishes academic discourse is not "the intellectual stance"—the "deep structure"—but "certain stylistic or mechanical conventions." Acknowledging that there are recognizable common features of generic academic style, Elbow goes on to investigate the "problematic intellectual and social implications" attending those conventions. He concludes that teachers should avoid teaching any "currently privileged set of stylistic conventions of academic discourse" but that they should devote time to the larger exploration of voices and styles appropriate to communicating with various live audiences. He suggests that when students are engaged in the demanding intellectual tasks of giving reasons and evidence to think through problems of genuine interest they will develop the conventions of "voice, register, tone, diction, syntax, and mannerisms" that will be effective with their audiences.

The same question of the intellectual and social implications of privileging the conventions of particular discourse communities Elbow discusses in connection with academic writing can be raised when considering the oral language used for classroom discussion and oral presentations. In oral language development as with writing, the goal is not that students learn one correct form of Standard English, and certainly not that they will see the language they bring into the school as inferior or wrong. Rather, we want our students to learn that different language forms are appropriate in different contexts. Lisa Delpit describes the process by which teachers help students acquire additional oral forms and points out the sensitivity that is required in the process.

> First, they should recognize that the linguistic form a student brings to school is intimately connected with loved ones, community, and personal identity. To suggest that this form is "wrong" or, even worse, ignorant, is to suggest that something is wrong with the student and his or her family. On the other hand, it is equally important to understand that students who do not have access to the politically popular dialect form in this country, i.e., Standard English, are less likely to succeed economically than their peers who do. (Delpit 1988a, 251)

There is a difference between providing students with opportunities to develop alternate language forms and insisting that the students change their own language. Delpit argues that teachers can only provide students with the knowledge base to decide when and how to use alternative language forms; the decision about which form to use in any context ultimately rests with the speaker.

A consideration of literary conventions and the conventions of academic and nonacademic discourse across the range of language functions should remind educators of the huge scope of the concept of conventions as an indicator of the level of the individual's language proficiencies and of the social and political implications implied in privileging particular conventions. At the same time, instructors shouldn't overlook the fact that included in these conventions are those mechanics teachers commonly associate with assessment. Grammar, usage, spelling, and punctuation do count in the academic world. Indeed, they are a major concern to those critics of education who see lapses in grammar and spelling by recent graduates as proof of declining academic standards. Therefore, teachers do a disservice to our students and to the community if these elements are ignored just as when they are overemphasized. The conventions of Standard English are important to performance in those language outcomes that are public in nature. In informational and critical writing and speech, control of the conventions of Standard English is essential to even minimally acceptable adult performance.

Independence

Independence is a problematic term in the present context of educational discussion. For many people, the term *independence* suggests the ability to perform without consultation or collaboration of any type. The perennial concern of teachers in grading written assignments is determining that the work handed in is really the student's own work. While many teachers have rejected the view that the only valid indicator of a student's ability is work produced without intervention or assistance of any kind and now recognize that human endeavor is usually collaborative and social, there is still a concern for determining how much personal control and responsibility the student demonstrates in learning and language use.

The question of "cheating"—of submitting someone else's work as one's own—is less of an issue in a classroom in which the process of making meaning through transactions among students, teachers, and texts constitutes the curriculum. In such a class teachers are constantly observing how students use language to make meaning. Assessment of student learning is a continuous process of observing their goals, what resources they call on, and how successfully they accomplish their goals. In such a classroom, independence takes on a different meaning from what it has had traditionally. Independence doesn't mean an absence of reliance on outside resources but responsibility, resourcefulness, and authority in selecting and using appropriate resources. Seen from this perspective, independence is a positive indicator of increasing capability, which moves teachers out of the deficit model of assessment that takes any evidence of a student's use of outside help as a mark of inadequacy and uses instead the same evidence to determine how successful the student is in using available resources in the process of finding and expressing meaning. The key elements are that the student's own thinking is evident throughout and that resources are used for the support or verification of that thinking.

Determining the amount of independence in student performance is complicated by the fact that school performances are often intentionally planned to include a great amount of teacher and peer assistance. Following Vygotsky's (1962) principle that "instruction is only useful when it moves ahead of development," teachers design classroom experiences that allow the student "to do in collaboration today [what] he will be able to do independently tomorrow" (211). Therefore, classroom projects and writing assignments are often the first, or nearly the first, of their kind that students have attempted. Even in cases in which the writing or project is similar in form to others students have done many times before, instructors expect that in some way each performance will represent a new level of challenge or accomplishment. It would be an ineffective use of school time for students to be asked to perform regularly at a level already within their mature functioning. Therefore, even in the case of writing or oral performance in forms long included within the student's repertoire, educators should look for evidence of new growth in the range and complexity of student demonstrations as meaning makers. Within this classroom context, complete independence in student performance would be an indication that the student was not operating at a sufficiently challenging level to provide opportunity for growth.

Since the discussion of independence in language performance is concerned primarily with school performance, it is important to consider more closely the issue of plagiarism. How do educators develop in students the ability to make use of the published ideas of others in ways that are legitimate and supportive? The best advice I have found on the question comes from Ann Berthoff (1981), who recommends the use of the double-entry notebook in which the student transcribes sections from the reading on one side of the page and annotates them on the other (writing summaries, comparisons, questions, arguments). The notebook forces students to think about transcribed material and its relationship to developing personal meaning so that the ideas or even the passages themselves find their way into the student writing (if they do) as examples or support or counterarguments, not in place of the student's own thinking. As teachers, we monitor our students' composing process and can see how well they are "progressing in learning to think critically, to see relationships methodically, to discover and develop meanings" (122), and we can intervene to help in that process.

All of this suggests that independence is not an either/or condition but a matter of degree. How independent are students in establishing their own purposes, in finding resources to accomplish those purposes, in deciding what is personally significant, and in selecting from a variety of available options? The mature thinker and language user does not operate in isolation but makes effective use of appropriate resources while maintaining the integrity of his or her own thinking.

Summary

The characteristics of performance useful for distinguishing degrees of proficiency in language use are not unique to language performance but are common factors in the description of performances of many types. Increases in range, flexibility, the ability to make connections, the control of conventions, and the degree of independence are evidence of growth in every area of human endeavor. As indicators of increasing proficiency in language performance they apply to particular elements.

Range

- *Meaning:* The scope of the expertise, including the dimensions of breadth and depth. For young people whose language performance is developing, the opportunity to explore a broad range is as important as depth in chosen areas.
- *Evidence:* Disciplines and subjects and topics within disciplines; cultures, historical periods, and genres of literature; modes and forms of writing; and registers of language.

Flexibility

- *Meaning:* The ability to perform in varied and changing conditions. Flexibility can only be developed or assessed when students have opportunities to use and analyze language in diverse contexts.
- *Evidence:* Ease of adaptation, consistency of quality of performance, control of all aspects of performance, awareness of demands of audience and purpose.

Connections

- *Meaning:* The ability to see commonalities in apparently disparate experiences or contexts and to apply already learned concepts to the widest range of data.
- *Evidence:* Use of analogies—logical connections with similar or closely related concepts; metaphors—imaginative connections with dissimilar concepts; and concrete examples of abstract concepts.

Conventions

- *Meaning:* The protocols, traditional practices, rules, skills, and other devices over which the individual has control.
- *Evidence:* Pragmatic: accommodation to aspects of the situation including demands of audience and purpose; rhetorical: accommodation to the expected features of the discourse; and

cultural: respect for customs of the group, whether determined by gender, ethnicity, profession, or common interest.

Independence

- *Meaning:* The ability to select, plan, execute, and monitor
  one's own performance without reliance on the direction of
  others.
- *Evidence:* Control of purpose—decides what to do and how
  to do it; use of resources — finds the help needed to accomplish the purpose and uses those resources effectively and
  honestly; and individual perspective—personal views, language, and style dominate.

Chapter Three

A Continuum of Standards

One of the consequences of the increasing popularity of the process curriculum in language education—a popularity which is evident in classrooms called "whole language," "response based," or "reading-writing workshops"—is the recognition that the language functions that students demonstrate as seniors are the same ones used throughout the grades. Thus many language arts syllabi are K–12 documents with provision for reading, writing, listening, and speaking for the same functions at every grade level. This approach to curriculum makes sense to teachers who reject the view that language development progresses in a sequential, linear fashion with more challenging forms being tackled after simpler forms are "mastered." Just as little children invent and tell stories even before they speak in full sentences, so do young students in elementary schools write stories and reports long before their teachers have had a chance to teach them the paragraph. Language learning can't be confined to an orderly scope and sequence chart that allows teachers to check off each component skill as it is demonstrated until eventually language itself has been mastered.

If language improves dynamically through use throughout school, how do we as teachers evaluate student performance at different grade levels or individuals at different levels of adult proficiency? How do we know what is good enough? How do we distinguish between acceptable report writing for a fourth-grade student and for a graduating senior?

For the many teachers who are uncomfortable about defining outcomes and standards for language arts, the real stumbling block is the idea of an assessment scale. The concept of putting language performance, with all its possibilities for rich, dynamic, individual, and creative expression, on a scale with levels of performance defined by specific criteria is abhorrent. I hope the preceding chapters have helped convince doubters that it is possible to articulate as outcomes and standards the language processes so many English teachers value. In *Embracing Contraries*, Peter Elbow (1986) considers the difficulty of expressing the "*deep* goals of *true* education" as outcomes. After considering the possibility that "metaphorical ability," "tolerance for ambiguity," and "virtue" are inimical to such definition, he concludes, "I end up suspecting, then, that there is nothing one cannot adopt as an educational goal or outcome, but that certain goals must be worked toward with great tact and intelligence, and others with a wise indirection" (135). Some methods of working toward the slippery language outcomes appear in the section on curriculum. For now, relying on Elbow's conclusion that an outcomes approach to language learning is not limiting, I want to consider how language outcomes at different levels of development might be described.

In describing outcomes performance, educators commonly refer to a continuum of performance from rudimentary to the highest possible level. The use of the term *continuum* indicates that the evaluation refers to the same outcome, whether the early stages or a very advanced performance. A continuum has two important dimensions: continuity and progression. The continuity is found in the common essential characteristics of the outcome that identify it; for example, the essential characteristics of reading for aesthetic response are the focus on personal responses and associations combined with attention to textual elements. The progression depends on those external variable factors that increase or decrease across the continuum. The variable factors I consider above are range, flexibility, connections, control of conventions, and independence. The continuum indicates the relative strength of an outcome. A common practice in everyday life in our society is to rate nearly everything on a scale from one to ten. A continuum differs from a simple numerical scale in that it indicates at particular points the criteria for performance at that level.

The continuum is an attempt to describe performance as it relates to the most exemplary model of a given behavior. If we start with the model of the superstars in the field as the reference point, other levels can be established that describe performances of lesser but still acceptable quality.

A four-level continuum of adult proficiency offers the possibility of making useful distinctions. Whether generic terms like "acceptable," "good," "very good," and "outstanding" are used or terms that suggest incremental stages like "beginner," "intermediate," "advanced," and "master," improving performance relative to an agreed upon scale that applies to all performers regardless of age can be described. Using a continuum seems strange to educators who are used to making norm-referenced judgments of student performance, such as formal measures that describe their students' performance with reference to "grade levels," (some seventh graders may be judged to read on a third-grade reading level and others on a twelfth-grade reading level). Many educators also make informal judgments based on their own expectations for students of a particular age or grade. Some students' writing may seem "outstanding" for seventh grade, for example, while others' is "not acceptable." It will take some adjusting for teachers (and students and parents) to think of student performance relative to a fixed scale, but experience in other areas of life may help.

A personal example may explain what I mean. At the age of thirty-seven I decided to learn to swim, in spite of a lifetime fearing water and a determined avoidance of any athletic activity. Like all nonswimmers I was assigned to a beginning level course. Instruction and practice centered on the same activities that the four- to six-year-old nonswimmers engaged in: blowing bubbles, kicking from the side of the pool, and trying to float. I don't know if the pace of instruction was more accelerated than in the class for small children, but I know that at the end of the six-week course I had acquired enough skill to be called a "beginning" swimmer. For a while after that I swam regularly—summer and winter—for exercise. Although no one was assessing my progress, I think I improved enough to be considered an advanced beginner.

There are a few important points to notice in this example. First, there is an enormous difference between being a nonswimmer, who is someone who lacks the ability to swim, and a swimmer, who is someone who possesses that ability at however rudimentary a level. Second, there is a difference between being a person who swims, even if infrequently, and one who doesn't swim, even if that person once learned and is still presumably able. A person who never swims is not considered to be a swimmer. Third, formal instruction is only part of acquiring any outcome; experience is an even greater factor in developing proficiency. My formal instruction in swimming consisted of those six weeks of daily one-hour lessons that resulted in my being able to stay afloat and do some elementary strokes to keep moving through the water. Improving those abilities and adding others to them was entirely the result of swimming regularly and observing and analyzing my own and other swimmers' performance. Fourth, the level of proficiency an individual achieves depends on expectations and determination. I decided to learn to swim so I could overcome a crippling fear and so I could exercise. Once I learned a couple of elementary strokes and improved them to the point that I could sustain them for enough time and distance to provide valuable exercise (and, importantly, perform in a way that would not humiliate me in the presence of other swimmers), I was content. My niece, on the other hand, who took her first lessons at the same time I did (but in the four-year-old group) has continued to take lessons at advanced levels, swims on a swim team, has a personal coach, and is constantly working on her swimming so she can compete at increasingly challenging levels.

The swimming example illustrates the significance of each part of the definition of outcomes as the knowledge and skills individuals can and do habitually demonstrate as a result of instruction and experience. Attainment of requisite skills is essential to the achievement and demonstration of any outcome. You don't move from the category of nonswimmer to that of swimmer unless you can stay afloat and propel yourself through water. But—and this is the crucial point—ability is not enough. Equally essential to achievement and demonstration of the outcome is use. Anyone who doesn't swim is considered a nonswimmer regardless of having demonstrated that ability at one time. We might say of such a person that she used to swim or is a former swimming star. Both *can* and *do* are important to the definition.

The swimming example also suggests that in most outcomes knowledge, skills, and attitudes are inextricable. Swimming, which is most obviously a skill, is only acquired by experience; I learned to swim by swimming, and there is no other way to learn. At the same time, knowledge of the strokes and conventions of swimming is necessary (but not sufficient) for performance as a swimmer, even though that knowledge may be tacit rather than conscious. Some conscious analysis of the rules or practices involved, through reflection on one's own performance and through observation and analysis of the performance of others, will certainly facilitate improvement.

Habitual performance also implies the willing engagement of the individual. I'm not a swimmer because I once passed a swimming test or a pianist because I successfully played "Fur Elise" in a high school recital or a writer because I have passed the state competency exam. I'm a swimmer, pianist, or writer only if I engage in that activity regularly. Such willing engagement signifies a positive attitude toward the activity (not necessarily enjoyment) and is an indication of its value for the individual. I write regularly by choice and feel a sense of absence when I'm not working on a piece of writing, but I can't say that I "enjoy" writing. Choosing to do it for my own purposes is all the proof I can offer of a positive attitude toward it.

Both instruction and experience are important for achievement of an outcome. Interestingly, the amount and nature of instruction is a factor that seems to vary more from one learner to another. Although it may seem that individuals with talent would want and need less formal instruction than beginners, the opposite is often true. Few people can reach or maintain their desired levels of performance without continuing experience, however. The amount of regular experience or practice varies considerably, but continued use is almost always essential.

Positive attitude, instruction, and experience are contributors to an individual's *process* in improving performance. They are essential factors to keep in mind when planning learning experiences. But in describing the criteria for assessing outcomes, I am concerned with factors that describe the performance itself, which are the essential components of the outcome and the characteristics of performance: range, flexibility, connections, conventions, and independence.

The Appendix contains continua for the language outcomes with eight levels of performance described for each outcome. The four highest points on the continua describe levels of adult performance from acceptable to outstanding. The first four levels are early developmental stages, which are useful for monitoring an individual's progress toward attainment of a desirable level of performance. The specific criteria on those continua can be useful for making determinations of the performance levels of students in each of the outcomes. They also may help us as educators to see that any individual's language proficiencies vary across the outcomes. Some students who are very good at the kind of meaning making involved in reading for information may be only acceptable at reading for aesthetic response and good at writing for critical analysis.

Criteria are one way of insuring that instructors have some common understanding of the levels. Another way is to try to describe in general terms the kind of habitual performance that might be seen at each level of these language outcomes. In the sections that follow I suggest a few examples for each level. The levels are so large and diverse that any number of equally valid examples might be found.

Aesthetic

Reading for Aesthetic Response

We all know readers who claim to read "everything and anything" in their personal reading. Actually only a few **outstanding readers** can read with ease in all the literary texts written in (or translated into) their language. Whether reading an extremely complex and enigmatic work like *Finnegans Wake* or Borges' *Labyrinths* or poems intended for children, outstanding readers are able to produce coherent readings of these texts that make sense of all (or at least most) of the textual elements and make insightful connections between the text and their own experiences. They have read so widely that each newly encountered text is understood in the context of other texts of similar genre or theme or cultural tradition.

Many of these outstanding readers are professional reviewers or writers of literature or literary scholars who seem to view literary texts almost as puzzles to be solved and who not only can fill in many gaps in the text to produce a rich reading but also are aware of gaps that aren't accounted for in their reading. They know that every text is open to many readings and interpretations and seem automatically to select from the possibilities to create the most satisfying reading. Their vast experience of literature enables them to recognize uses and violations of conventions such as archetypal themes and imagery, traditional structures, or characterization, and to respond to or resist these elements in their reading. Their authority is such that many other readers will accept their reading of a text as more insightful than that of the author. For example, when John Updike reviews the first novel of a young writer and finds humor where the author had intended tragedy or cites influences the writer was not even conscious of, many readers of the review may accept Updike's reading because of their respect for his literary genius. They do not say Updike got it wrong.

Not as authoritative or as all encompassing in their reading are **very good** literary readers who read widely and deeply in all genres. These readers may also be teachers of literature, members of literary discussion groups, or readers for whom reading literature is more than just an occasional way to pass time. Their preference in literature may be for texts that are more demanding than popular works. They are able to find ways into everything they read and have a wide range of experience with literature that helps them recognize significant textual elements and raise crucial questions for themselves and other readers. They know a great deal about literary conventions and use what they know to produce a satisfying reading of the text that makes sense of textual elements and their own responses. In discussions of literature the responses of these readers cause other readers to see and understand patterns and symbolism that other readers hadn't noticed.

Good readers for aesthetic response choose to read literature of many kinds for their own enjoyment. While the range of literature that they read may not be as extensive as that of more proficient readers, there may be some genres or topics or authors in which they read very deeply and in which they are quite expert. There are groups of readers who meet to share readings of favorite poetry or to discuss historical or regional fiction or mystery novels or writings by and about a favorite author. These readers bring to readings of these texts a breadth of understanding that gives them considerable authority in discovering recurring themes, images, and characters as well as variations across texts. In reading literature of unfamiliar kinds they can draw on their previous literary and life experiences to find some commonalities and to construct meaning, though it may be a relatively limited one. They may be more successful in recognizing and responding sensitively to common human experiences in literature than in appreciating the significant differences.

Acceptable readers for aesthetic response may read from a limited range of texts for their own enjoyment, perhaps only popular literature or the literature of one or two genres. Within that range they can recognize common themes and connect their own experiences with aspects of the text in order to understand the text more fully. They know some literary conventions and use them to help themselves predict and interpret events as the text unfolds. When reading required literature in school, they may rely on help from the teacher to recognize significant aspects of the text and to produce a successful reading. Some readers in this category will increase their range and the complexity of their responses as they continue to gain literary experience; others may prefer to continue reading only the limited range of texts that appeal to them and will not branch out into more complex literature.

Writing for Aesthetic Response and Expression

Outstanding writers for aesthetic response and expression are those who produce beautiful works of art. This is the category of great writers of literature: Shakespeare, Milton, Austen, and Brontë as well as William Faulkner, Toni Morrison, Adrienne Rich, Ishmael Reed, E.B. White, Katherine Paterson, Madeleine L'Engle, and Dr. Seuss. But this category of writers also includes those responders and reviewers who produce insightful readings of literature that convey their lived-through experience of a text so effectively their reading becomes in itself a compelling literary experience. Hazlitt's response to *Hamlet* ("Whoever has become thoughtful and melancholy through his own mishaps or those of others . . . this is the true Hamlet") and Keats' sonnet "On First Looking into Chapman's Homer" are themselves works of art to which readers in turn respond aesthetically. Although these writers may be known primarily as masters of a particular genre, they demonstrate an understanding of a vast range of literary conventions and human experiences and a distinctive style that is recognized by others and often imitated.

Very good writers for aesthetic response and expression are those professional writers and serious amateurs whose writing is effective and pleasing in style and content but lacking the originality of the outstanding professionals. Many writers of popular fiction and poetry fall into this group. Their works demonstrate great control of literary conventions and an effective style and personal vision but for the most part they are writing within established traditions rather than breaking new ground. Responders and reviewers of this level produce insightful and compelling readings of a wide range of literary works, but their responses are not works of art in themselves as were those of Keats and Hazlitt in the examples above.

Good writers for aesthetic response and expression use a considerable range of literary forms to write for particular purposes. They may write poems to celebrate family occasions, stories to read to their own children or their students, parodies of classical or popular works to entertain friends, or diaries, journals, or chronicles of their own experiences. In their responses and reviews of literature they make clear personal associations with the work, explaining their emotional responses to particular aspects of the text. They display an understanding of a variety of literary conventions and refer to them in their written responses. Their style is personal and appealing.

Acceptable writers for aesthetic response and expression have at least a few forms they use to express themselves. They may keep journals or diaries, write in free verse, compose lyrics for songs or raps, or write humorous anecdotes. Their mastery of literary conventions may be limited to those of a few traditional genres, and they may prefer to write in familiar forms rather than to experiment with new ones, relying to a great extent on models or the help of more experienced writers. Their writing may be formulaic but clear and coherent. Their responses and reviews of literature indicate a limited range of knowledge of conventions and subject matter and may deal primarily with the surface-level meaning of the work. They are, however, effective in explaining their personal associations with the text in clear and specific language.

Listening and Speaking for Aesthetic Response and Expression

This category is complex, including a variety of oral language situations: listening for aesthetic response to the performances of others, expressing orally aesthetic responses, and giving oral performances of an artistic nature.

The group of **outstanding** listeners for aesthetic response includes film, theater, and opera reviewers and commentators who are able to produce insightful responses and interpretations to almost any oral performance in their language. Like the outstanding aesthetic readers, they bring a vast experience of dramatic performances to each new experience and respond to the newly encountered from the context of other performances of similar genre, theme, or cultural tradition, and they have the same authority in their responses and reviews.

Outstanding speakers for aesthetic response and expression perform moving dramatic presentations. Some of them are professional actors who perform in theater and film and whose performances set the standard for other performers (Olivier in *Hamlet,* and Vanessa Redgrave in *Playing for Time*) or humorists who entertain audiences with their monologues (Mark Twain is an early example; late-night talk show hosts are a contemporary example). Others are professional storytellers or performers of dramatic literature whose readings and oral presentations bring the literature alive and make their interpretation of it clear and compelling.

Very good listeners for aesthetic response include those dedicated theater or film or opera buffs who may not make a living reviewing dramatic performances but whose wide range of experience enables them to follow a performance with ease, drawing on their prior experience and their knowledge of the conventions to construct a satisfying meaning. In discussions they are able to make sense of many elements of the performance. Very good speakers for aesthetic response and expression may be amateur or professional performers whose performances are modeled on the examples of the great performers (such as imitating Laurence Olivier's performance of Hamlet rather than interpreting the role in a unique way). They are often also teachers, storytellers, and community performers whose oral performances and public readings of poetry and stories or dramatic monologues or religious texts effectively convey the meaning and the feeling of the works to a wide variety of audiences.

Good listeners for aesthetic response frequently attend oral performances of a variety of types. They may prefer popular performances to more serious art forms for the most part and may rely on the guidance of experienced reviewers when listening to performances of unfamiliar types. However, they may enjoy sophisticated performances of a few areas of special interest, such as films or plays on a topic of personal interest (baseball or war, for example) or all the work of a particular performer or genre (musical comedy) and, as a result, they may be quite expert in that area. As speakers, these individuals may tell stories or jokes or recite favorite pieces for family gatherings; they may give readings for local community groups; they may be known among their acquaintances as entertaining conversationalists. Their oral presentations may not show insight into the complexity of the meaning or emotional content of the work and they may not be able to speak before an audience of people they do not know, but they demonstrate ease and poise in performing favorite selections for their acquaintances.

Acceptable listeners for aesthetic response attend a limited range of oral performances for their own enjoyment. They may prefer popular films, television shows, and performers but may listen to serious dramatic presentations only when required to as part of a course of study. In their responses to popular performances they are familiar with, they use their understanding of the conventions of those genres to follow the presentations, to anticipate what is coming, and to recognize the humor or emotion of the work. In their responses to more sophisticated performances, they may rely on the prompting and modeling of a teacher to recognize significant aspects of the performance and to construct a satisfactory meaning. As speakers for aesthetic expression, these individuals may be quite limited in their range of presentations and in the audiences for whom they will perform. They may tell stories to young children or jokes to their peers or may read passages from literature or scriptures to elderly or infirm acquaintances, but they may be unwilling to perform more publicly. In required performances of a more formal nature, such as the recitation of a monologue or a dramatic reading for a class, they can perform adequately with proper direction, enunciating clearly and conveying a coherent sense of the work.

Informational

Reading for Information and Understanding

Like the category of outstanding readers for aesthetic response, the category of **outstanding** readers for information and understanding includes scholars who spend their lives reading and studying. These scholars read extensively in the professional material of their own disciplines first and foremost, but in order to understand the relationship of their discipline to all other knowledge they read widely beyond their own particular area of expertise. They have enormous prior knowledge of the subjects they are reading about and rely on that knowledge to make decisions about the significance, validity, and value of information they find in new texts. They read diverse material with authority and confidence, going to the text for their own purposes, abstracting information they need to support a position or to solve a problem, ignoring information that is not relevant, and assigning relative significance to different information based on what they already know. They use an enormous variety of printed material to find information that they want: charts, maps, logs, account books, diaries, riddles, poems, as well as expository text from the straightforward to the highly esoteric. Other readers respect their expertise and accept their interpretations as authoritative.

Very good readers for information and understanding also demonstrate considerable authority over texts on a wide range of subject matter. Like the outstanding readers, they read extensively in disciplines beyond their own particular specialization but may not read as deeply in all areas. They may be teachers or professionals in a discipline who read regularly the technical material and professional publications of that discipline and understand the current debates going on among those professionals. Within their own discipline they have a great deal of knowledge that enables them to assign significance and to make decisions about the validity of newly encountered information. A broad base of general knowledge enables them to see issues of common concern across disciplines and to use their understanding from one area to help them understand information in another. They are respected for informed and thorough readings of scholarly texts in their own and related disciplines but don't have the same authority as the outstanding scholars, on whom they may rely for models and guidance.

Good readers for information and understanding read widely in texts of many disciplines to acquire information for their own purposes. They may read mostly in texts written for a general audience rather than highly technical materials or professional journals, but in areas of special interest they can and do read complex and sophisticated texts. They decide for themselves what information is significant or valuable for their purposes and make use of a variety of materials, including charts and graphics. They have a considerable knowledge base in at least a few specialized areas and can use their previous understanding to help them make sense of new information. They know what resources are available for finding information in their areas of interest and can use those resources efficiently.

At the **acceptable** level, readers for information and understanding may be rather limited in the range of disciplines as well as in the type of material they read. For their independent reading, they may confine themselves to texts written for the general public and may be able to find information in more specialized material only with the help of a more experienced reader. They have a general understanding of current affairs and read in popular magazines and newspapers to increase their knowledge of topics found there, and they can read the manuals and informational material included in consumer products to obtain information about assembly, use, care, or hazards. In areas of special interest to their chosen occupation or field of academic study, they can find and use more specialized and complex material to obtain information and can make decisions about the significance and value of information with the help of people more experienced in that field.

Writing for Information and Understanding

Outstanding writers for information and understanding may, to a great extent, be the same individuals who are outstanding readers for information and understanding. Within every discipline scholars, essayists, and journalists read each other's contributions to the conversations going on in their field and contribute their own written opinions. The outstanding writers contribute new understanding to the ongoing conversation. The tradition of conferring doctoral degrees rests on the requirement that candidates must contribute some new teaching or understanding to that field, which doesn't mean that every person who has earned a doctorate is an outstanding writer in that field; only those who *habitually* write on issues of significance to their discipline and whose writing continues to advance the understanding of those issues are in the category of outstanding writers. Most writers at this level are scholarly writers who publish their writing in a very narrow specialty and are regarded as leading authorities in that specialty. In writing for other professionals in the field, they use language and conventions respected by members of that profession. However, other writers in this category may be commentators on a broad range of issues and disciplines who provide public information on a great variety of topics. Their genius lies in being able to take sophisticated ideas from all these areas and to write about them in language that makes the ideas accessible to the general public.

Very good writers for information and understanding also write with authority on issues within their professional disciplines or their areas of interest or academic study. They may write most often to make sense of ideas propounded by other thinkers in the field or to apply someone else's ideas or theories to a particular situation or to make sophisticated ideas accessible to a general audience rather than contributing significant new thinking to the discussion in their field of interest, as outstanding writers do. These writers may write for professional journals or conferences or for popular magazines or newspapers. Their most sophisticated writing may be on topics of interest to their particular specialty, but they can also write effectively on a wide range of topics of general interest or for academic investigation in a variety of disciplines. They have broad-based knowledge from which they draw analogies or metaphors that make complex information comprehensible to a wider audience. They understand the conventions of each discipline in which they write and use those conventions effectively.

Good writers for information and understanding write to explain and explore information necessary for their work, study, or personal affairs. In work situations they may write required reports, using prescribed formats and language. In academic study they write clear and coherent explanations of ideas and information in each discipline they study, drawing their information from textbooks, from publications for general adult audiences, and perhaps from some specialized professional journals or publications. Their writing follows the conventions of standard written English and shows some accommodation to the particular discourse conventions of the disciplines they are investigating. In their personal affairs they write to communicate with businesses and with community and political agencies for a wide range of purposes using accepted forms (business letters, memos, abstracts), Standard English, and language and diction appropriate for the audience.

Acceptable writers for information and understanding write in similar forms for work, study, and personal affairs as the good writers. These writers, however, often rely on models or prescriptions or the guidance of others to help them present information in acceptable forms. In the workplace they may follow an outline or sample to prepare reports, inserting specific information into a standard format. In academic study they may work with a teacher or writing group in order to report or explain information in appropriate language and forms. They use Standard English correctly and know some acceptable ways of organizing information. In writing for personal affairs they use accepted business letter form, Standard English, and appropriate language.

Listening and Speaking for Information and Understanding

The **outstanding** category of listeners and speakers for information and understanding includes individuals who attend and present lectures at professional conferences and public forums and those who participate in panel discussions or other formal oral investigations of technical or scholarly topics. As listeners, these individuals bring an enormous wealth of prior knowledge to these discussions and focus their attention selectively on new elements or on those that support or challenge their own understanding of the topic. As speakers they present new information for the contemplation of the audience and new ways of looking at existing information. Their presentational strategies, poise, organization, and delivery make their thinking compelling to an audience of their fellow professionals. Some listeners and speakers of this category are able to listen to assess the level of understanding of an audience and to present complex information in a way that is accessible to that audience. Others are brilliant in presenting original thinking to peers but are not able to adjust their presentations for general audiences.

Very good listeners and speakers for information and understanding engage in professional discussions of complex issues and ideas in their field. They may attend conferences or lectures or business meetings where highly technical or sophisticated information is presented and they are able to acquire that information and recognize its significance. They also use their broad-based knowledge to acquire and understand information on a great range of issues of general interest. As speakers they present complex information effectively for a variety of audiences. In this category of very good listeners and speakers for information and understanding are the best teachers at every level from early childhood to university who present large amounts of complex information comprehensibly to audiences of students not yet expert in the disciplines they are studying. These teachers have the ability to present the same information in many different ways, from different perspectives, and in understandable language.

Good listeners and speakers for information and understanding participate in discussions of important issues from a wide range of disciplines. As listeners they are able to acquire complex and sophisticated information from formal lectures and presentations and from discussions with a great variety of people. They have a broad base of knowledge on topics of current issues and in a number of academic areas that they use to understand new information on topics of personal interest. As speakers they can present information on areas of particular interest clearly and effectively for general audiences. They use language forms appropriate to a wide range of audiences, from informal language with friends and family to Standard English for general audiences to more specialized language for academic discussion within a particular discipline or profession.

Acceptable listeners and speakers for information and understanding participate in discussions of issues of personal concern related to their chosen occupation, field of study, and community involvement. As listeners they are able to acquire and understand information from formal presentations aimed at the general public, from classroom lectures and discussions for entry-level college students, and from discussions with coworkers and with members of their community. As speakers they can explain information related to their jobs or to their area of study or personal interest clearly and coherently for audiences of family, friends, and coworkers. They speak confidently in informal language with close associates and can switch to Standard English for discussion with business contacts or community representatives.

Critical

Reading for Critical Analysis and Evaluation

In describing the other language outcomes it has been difficult to avoid slipping into a description of critical language use. All significant language use is critical in that the individual is always standing in a particular perspective and selecting particular aspects of an experience to respond to or study. The group of **outstanding** readers for critical analysis and evaluation includes professional literary critics as well as scholars of other disciplines who analyze texts from the perspective of their particular discipline. These readers are similar to outstanding readers in each of the other categories, but their readings differ from the others in that rather than being interpretive or explanatory these readings are evaluative. Critical readings of professional publications evaluate texts according to particular criteria. These readers speak on behalf of a group of which they are members and make clear in their readings the values of the group on which their criteria are founded. They have a vast understanding of the different perspectives and value systems of other groups. Like the outstanding readers in other categories, their authority is recognized by members of their discipline and their evaluations are widely admired and accepted.

Very good readers for critical analysis and evaluation also bring a solid understanding of the assumptions and values of the cultural group for whom they speak. These readers may also publish their critical readings of texts, but those published critiques may lack the extensive connections to the field and may be more narrowly focused on the immediate context. For example, a local newspaper commentator might critique a recently published text on the tensions in the

Middle East based on a personal understanding of recent events there and individual political values and assumptions while a political scientist might base a critique on the system of professional values, a much broader understanding of the histories and competing philosophies of all of the peoples of the region, and knowledge of similar conflicts in other regions and at other times. Many readers of this category are teachers who analyze significant texts written by leading thinkers of a discipline and make connections for their students between a text and the field in general. They have a broad base of general knowledge that allows them to analyze each text from a number of perspectives and to articulate their analyses comprehensibly to less-knowledgeable audiences.

Good readers for critical analysis and evaluation read widely in publications for general audiences on topics of current interest, in the literature of a variety of genres, and in texts related to areas of particular personal interest, and they analyze the texts they read from a variety of different perspectives. They have general knowledge of many perspectives on current issues and can analyze and judge a text from one perspective while recognizing alternative evaluations of the same text from other perspectives. For example, a member of the Democratic party might analyze an article by William F. Buckley on unemployment from the vantage point of party beliefs about the proper role of government, while at the same time being aware of the different analysis of the text that would be made by members of the Republican party. These individuals read to form their own opinions on issues of concern to them in political, social, ethical, and business matters and are aware of the value systems and criteria by which they form their judgments. In reading and analyzing literature they know some traditional criteria for evaluating literary quality as well as a variety of social and cultural perspectives for assessing the relevance and validity of literary works.

The **acceptable** readers for critical analysis and evaluation read and analyze publications for general audiences and literature of a variety of genres. These readers have general knowledge of current issues and of conflicting perspectives on those issues, and they understand the perspectives of groups with which they identify on many issues and the values and beliefs on which those positions are based. In reading texts on complex issues and unfamiliar topics, these readers may generally rely on the analyses of other thinkers to help them form their judgments. They may, for example, read critical reviews of literature to help them analyze the work and form their own evaluation of it or rely on class lectures and discussions of academic reading to formulate an analysis of it. They may be aware that there are many different perspectives on any text but may tend to form judgments based on their own personal concerns. In evaluating literature they may use personal criteria for what makes a good story rather than the criteria studied in school for literary analysis, and in evaluating articles in newspapers and magazines they may be more concerned with how those texts reflect the values of their family and friends rather than with the ideology of a more abstract collective (the nation, the party, the church). However, in their academic study they will analyze texts from particular perspectives with the guidance of a teacher.

Writing for Critical Analysis and Evaluation

The group of **outstanding** writers for critical analysis and evaluation includes those scholars who publish their analyses of the writings of other scholars in their field in a sort of public dialogue, but also those writers who write regularly on issues of current concern as spokespersons for a particular group and whose authority is accepted and respected by the group. This category includes not only the leading scholars of every academic discipline but also political commentators, feminist critics, gay rights activists, religious thinkers from fundamentalist to New Age, and so on. Outstanding critical writers contribute new insights and judgments that help others on significant issues. Other members of their group look to them for guidance on new issues and questions. These writers make complex analyses of difficult issues accessible to other members of their discipline or cultural group, and they are respected for the precision and style of their language as well as for the persuasiveness of their thinking.

Very good writers for critical analysis and evaluation may write analyses of current issues in popular publications for a general audience or for their professional colleagues. They differ from the outstanding writers of this category in that their analyses are not necessarily original but may synthesize the views of leading thinkers in a field and make that thinking available to people outside the group. They clearly articulate the criteria they use in their judgments and the group values on which they are based. They write clear and persuasive prose that convinces the audience of the validity of the judgment and the criteria. Newspaper editors who choose sides in a public debate and present arguments for their position, political activists who produce leaflets summarizing arguments on their side of an important issue, and academics who write papers and theses supporting a particular critical view of issues or texts may all be members of this category.

Good writers for critical analysis and evaluation formulate written judgments of issues of personal or professional concern and of issues related to their areas of academic study. They may write letters to the editor of the local newspaper or to local officials or business associates to persuade others of the justice of their position on an issue. In their writing they clarify the particular perspective they are taking, identifying themselves as members of particular interest groups (taxpayers, parents of children in the school, union members, leading salespeople) and clearly articulating the interests of the group in the issue. In academic writing they display an understanding of the different perspectives within the discipline they are studying and analyze issues from several of those perspectives using personally selected criteria. For example, in psychology class students may analyze a case study from Freudian, Jungian, and Ericksonian perspectives and within those perspectives they may choose to focus on particular criteria more than others in their assessment of the severity of the case. Their writing is clear and convincing and their arguments well structured.

Acceptable writers for critical analysis and evaluation write to persuade others of their view on issues of personal concern. They may write for the most part as required by their jobs or their academic study and with reliance on the guidance of employers or teachers. They may write occasional letters to the editor or to local government officials to express opinions on issues of particular concern to a group to which they belong. When writing analytical or evaluative pieces for their job or school, they apply criteria accepted in that context. Their writing is clear and coherent, and they can follow models or directions to produce sound analyses.

Listening and Speaking for Critical Analysis and Evaluation

The category of **outstanding** listeners and speakers for critical analysis and evaluation includes those people who engage in public debate on issues of significance to a group they represent. Diplomats, elected representatives, religious leaders, and social activists are found in this group as are those scholars who regularly participate in professional forums. These listeners can analyze the arguments of other speakers from the perspective of the group they themselves represent and can formulate counterarguments from that perspective. They can also understand the diverse perspectives of other cultural groups and the assumptions and values inherent in those perspectives. As speakers they present new insights on issues from the perspective of their social group. They provide cogent analyses of issues in language clarifying the underlying premises and values on which their arguments rest and acknowledging the differing values of other viewpoints. These speakers are recognized for the logic and authority of their arguments, complexity of their thinking, effectiveness of their presentation, and especially for their ability to suit their argument and delivery to the audience and the context.

Very good listeners and speakers for critical analysis and evaluation also engage in public debate on issues of significance to their social groups, but these individuals differ from the outstanding listeners and speakers principally in the originality of their positions. Whereas the outstanding category includes those who present unique analyses and insights to an issue, these listeners and speakers synthesize existing perspectives to formulate their positions. This category includes media commentators who listen to public debates in a variety of forums and present their analyses of the arguments for their audiences. It also includes teachers of every level and many students who synthesize their understandings of the issues from a variety of sources and present comprehensible analyses of the issues in their classes. They are able to analyze and evaluate issues from a variety of perspectives and explain the significance of an issue as it relates to different social groups.

Good listeners and speakers for critical analysis and evaluation participate in discussions on issues of interest to their social groups within their communities, their workplaces, and their schools. They listen to the public addresses of political, business, and religious leaders and form their own opinions on issues presented according to the value systems of their own social groups. They engage in discussion and debate on significant issues with their associates and present their analyses and evaluations clearly and convincingly, often supporting their positions through references to the opinions of recognized experts. These individuals have broad-based general knowledge that enables them to recognize a number of perspectives on issues of general concern.

Acceptable listeners and speakers for critical analysis and evaluation engage in the debate and discussion of issues of personal concern with close associates and will engage in more formal analyses of issues of academic or professional concern when directed by a teacher or supervisor. These individuals may form strong opinions of media presentations or public discussions of issues of immediate concern to their community and may present forceful arguments and evaluations of those issues in conversations in the community. They may acknowledge a number of different perspectives on the issues and be able to respond to arguments from several perspectives but may lack the broad general knowledge necessary to see issues in all the complexity that they have for more sophisticated critics. In their academic study or workplace they will investigate issues of importance with the direction of their teacher or supervisor and will present clear and well-constructed analyses according to established criteria.

Social Interaction

As we saw in the earlier discussion of language for social interaction, language used for social interaction is most immediately embedded in context and therefore is most often oral. For that reason I will start with a description of the levels of listening and speaking for social interaction and add a brief description of the levels of writing for social interaction. Keep in mind that this is the language that has for its primary function being with the other and, whether oral or written, aims at communicating the self more than a particular message.

Listening and Speaking for Social Interaction

At the **outstanding** level the category of listeners and speakers for social interaction includes those individuals who use social conversation to influence people across the broadest spectrum of diversity. In this category are many world leaders, diplomats, international businesspeople, and other professionals who in the course of their professional lives meet and converse with individuals of many countries and social classes. These individuals are able to influence others through the informal conversations they engage in outside of their official meetings. They are able to build goodwill and camaraderie in their talks over dinner tables, on the golf course, at weekend retreats, or in small talk between formal discussions. They rely on their wide cultural knowledge to respond sensitively to verbal and nonverbal signals. They communicate in a way that fosters trust and confidence, and they use language sensitive to the customs and expectations of others.

Very good listeners and speakers for social interaction are found in every profession and occupation and in every community. These are the individuals who can engage in conversation with the people they encounter each day, regardless of the diversity of those people, in a way that fosters goodwill and breaks down barriers. Doctors with excellent bedside manner who instill confidence and tranquility in their patients, teachers whose words make each child feel special and capable, employers who inspire loyalty and dedication in their employees, and workers who address customers and coworkers in friendly and compassionate ways are all in this category. These individuals, like those in the outstanding category, are knowledgeable and respectful of the customs and sensitivities of diverse people within their acquaintance. They convey an attitude of acceptance and respect in their verbal and nonverbal responses. They may be negotiators and go-betweens in internal disputes. They make good group leaders because of their ability to use language to influence others.

Good listeners and speakers for social interaction use language to promote goodwill and establish positive relations with people of their communities. They are effective in listening and speaking to establish good relationships with people with whom they come into daily contact in their neighborhoods or workplaces regardless of age, gender, ethnicity, or economic status. These individuals are respectful and polite in their conversation with people they meet in the larger society, but they may not be as comfortable or as effective in conversations with strangers. They know a variety of language forms and can use the language appropriate for a wide variety of social relationships and occasions.

Acceptable listeners and speakers for social interaction engage in conversation to establish and maintain good relationships with people in their homes, school, workplaces, and communities. These individuals may be open and confident in conversing only with people whom they know very well, but in those relationships they are able to express themselves effectively. In social interactions with strangers they may speak little but will listen to others attentively and respond respectfully when appropriate. They know enough language forms to converse appropriately with people of different ages and stations in life.

Writing for Social Interaction

Writing for social interaction is a proxy for being with the other; it is written down conversation. It does not differ substantially from the oral language use described above. The differences are found mostly in the forms of the communications.

Outstanding writers for social interaction are able to use social notes to establish and maintain positive relationships with extremely diverse professional and personal acquaintances. Like their speech, their writing conveys a message of personal sincerity and goodwill that inspires trust in the audience. These writers may be diplomats or professionals who send messages to others when they are at a distance. Their writing exhibits the same cultural sensitivity as their speech and respects cultural conventions for social correspondence. To the extent appropriate for the relationship and the culture, these writers write in personal, conversational language rather than in formal discourse.

Very good writers for social interaction use social notes to maintain positive professional and personal relationships with acquaintances from diverse groups within their own society. They send notes to mark important occasions in the lives of their acquaintances and include in the message personal references that convey sincere interest and feeling rather than pro forma greetings. They write in natural, informal language but use tone and diction appropriate to the relationship and to the culture of the audience.

Good writers for social interaction send notes to friends, family, and professional acquaintances within their communities. They write notes and letters to keep in touch with friends who are at a distance and send greetings to a larger circle of acquaintances to mark important occasions. This category also includes those individuals who write to intimates in order to express sentiments they are unable to express face to face—Cyrano's letters to Roxanne may be a good example, but personal letters may also fit—or to make a more lasting commemoration of an occasion (letters to a child upon a graduation or wedding day, thank you notes to parents on their wedding anniversary). These writers use language that is personal and distinctive and conveys to the audience the special nature of the relationship.

Acceptable writers for social interaction send notes to distant friends or relatives. They send personal greetings to friends and family members on important occasions. These individuals may write personal letters only to people within their circle of intimate acquaintances, but they send greetings of a more conventional nature to mark occasions in the lives of casual acquaintances or business associates.

Summary

A continuum for each of the language outcomes can be described by thinking of the standard setters in each of those areas and describing the performance of less-accomplished performers in terms relative to those standard setters.

Reading for Aesthetic Response and Expression

- *Standard Setters:* Professional reviewers, writers, and scholars of literature whose range of texts is virtually unlimited, whose prior literary and life experiences are vast and diverse, whose insights and connections are assured, and whose readings are original, complex, and authoritative.

Writing for Aesthetic Response and Expression

- *Standard Setters:* Writers of poetry, drama, fiction, and literary essays whose writing creates original forms or styles of writing or adds previously unknown dimensions to a genre.

Listening and Speaking for Aesthetic Response and Expression

- *Standard Setters:* Professional reviewers of performing arts whose commentaries are original, insightful, and authoritative. Professional actors, storytellers, and humorous and inspirational speakers whose performances give original insight into the emotional and intellectual content of material performed.

Reading for Information and Understanding

- *Standard Setters:* Scholars whose knowledge of their own discipline and of related areas is so vast so as to allow them to locate desired information and to decide the significance and validity of newly encountered information from an enormous variety of printed material.

Writing for Information and Understanding

- *Standard Setters:* Scholars whose writing contributes new knowledge and understanding to their disciplines as well as commentators who make sophisticated ideas from many disciplines accessible to the general public.

Listening and Speaking for Information and Understanding

- *Standard Setters:* Lecturers and presenters at professional conferences whose thinking and presentational strategies combine to contribute new thinking and understanding to the discipline as well as outstanding news commentators who make major developments in a great variety of fields accessible to the general public.

Reading for Critical Analysis and Evaluation

- *Standard Setters:* Professional literary critics as well as scholars of other disciplines who produce authoritative analyses of texts from the perspective of a particular professional or cultural group, confidently selecting and applying appropriate criteria according to the values of the group and the demands of the text, and whose analyses indicate a vast understanding of the perspectives and value systems of other groups.

Writing for Critical Analysis and Evaluation

- *Standard Setters:* Critics and scholars who publish their analyses of the writings of other scholars in the field in a public dialogue and whose analyses and judgments of issues of current concern to their field are considered by their peers to be authoritative and reliable.

Listening and Speaking for Critical Analysis and Evaluation

- *Standard Setters:* Those who engage in public debate on issues of significance in any field of public endeavor, whose views are well founded in the cultural tradition they represent, and who are respected for the cogency of their views and the effectiveness of their presentation.

Listening, Speaking, and Writing for Social Interaction

- *Standard Setters:* Diplomats and international business and professional people who use social conversation and written social messages to influence people and to establish and maintain harmonious relations with people from every culture and social class.

Finding Common Standards

The designation of standard setters for each of the categories and the above descriptions of the performers are certainly arguable. All of us as language users could suggest other examples of each category; many of us would argue that some examples included in a category do not fit, which I think is bound to be true when defining such large and diverse categories in such specific terms. However, the process of arguing about what examples should be included in each category is a useful one, and forces educators to think about personal internalized standards for each outcome. Ultimately, the purpose of describing the levels of performance for each of the outcomes is to give us a common understanding of the levels so we as teachers can have some confidence that we mean the same thing when describing our students' language performance on the continuum. How we might use the continuum for reporting the achievement of students is the subject of the next chapter.

Chapter Four

Standards, Benchmarks, and the Continuum

As the previous chapter suggests, for any defined outcome a continuum can be described with any number of designated levels of performance. Four levels of adult performance provide an adequate range for describing the proficiency of any mature language user and are useful for evaluating the achievements of graduating seniors. It is reasonable that a school would set a standard that requires all seniors to demonstrate performance at or above the acceptable adult level for each of the desired learning outcomes. One question that arises is how to indicate performance that falls below the acceptable adult level. To do that, levels of developing behavior as well as the levels of adult behavior are needed. The eight-level continuum in Figure 4-1 and the expanded description of the outcomes in the Appendix describe four levels of early developmental performance and four levels of mature functioning. A continuum that includes the developmental stages is useful in elementary and middle schools for monitoring students' progress toward the attainment of those outcomes expected at graduation as well as providing information about those high school seniors who have not yet achieved the desired level of proficiency.

The eight levels might be labeled as follows:

Level 1—beginning elementary
Level 2—independent elementary
Level 3—dependent intermediate
Level 4—independent intermediate
Level 5—minimal adult competency
Level 6—mature proficiency

Figure 4-1

Developmental Performance Scales on an Outcome Continuum

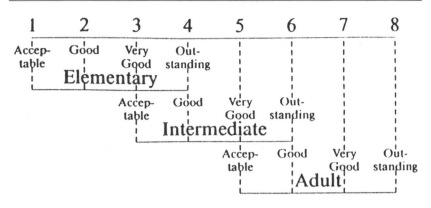

Level 7—exceptional proficiency

Level 8—standard-setting professional

I cannot stress enough the value of understanding the continuum as related to levels of performance rather than to age or grade expectations. Any person's habitual performance of an outcome can be designated by one of the levels regardless of age. An adult who is just learning to read might be performing at level 1 on the continuum for reading for information and understanding, just as a second grader might be. Keeping in mind the performance designations used in nonacademic areas might help make that distinction. As noted previously, people are referred to as "beginning swimmers" or "novice cooks" or as having an "elementary understanding" of some subject, regardless of age.

The four levels of mature performance (levels 5 through 8) enable instructors to indicate a considerable range of acceptable adult behavior. Four-level scales can also be used to indicate a comparable range of performance for developing stages. As Figure 4-1 indicates, the eight-level continuum yields three overlapping four-level scales that can be used at different stages in a student's development to indicate progress toward the standard. Levels 1 through 4 make up the elementary scale, levels 3 through 6 the intermediate scale, and levels 5 through 8 the adult scale. These scales can be used to assess the progress of any group of learners on the desired learning outcomes. The elementary scale might be used in a traditional school to assess the progress of all the fourth graders, the nine-year-olds, or the children who are ready to transfer to the middle school. It might also be used to assess the progress of adult learners who had completed the first session of an adult literacy program. The intermediate scale might be used in a traditional school to assess the progress of students about to enter the senior high school, but it might also be used in an adult literacy program to assess the progress of all students who had completed three sessions. The adult scale, as discussed in preceding chapters, can be used to certify the achievement of graduating seniors, but it is also useful as a means of describing the relative proficiency of all adults.

The relationships among the terms *outcomes, benchmarks, standards,* continuum *levels, criteria,* and *performance indicators* need to be sorted out. Sometimes these terms are used interchangeably, suggesting they mean the same thing, but sometimes these terms are used to convey somewhat different meanings. Therefore, I will try to sort out the exact meaning I am assigning to each term and then see how they might relate to each other.

At the beginning of this book I defined *outcomes* as the knowledge, skills, and understandings that individuals can and do habitually demonstrate as a result of instruction and experience. Outcomes may be stated in very general terms. For example, using the examples from nonacademic areas that we considered before, I might state as an outcome, "The individual swims," or "The individual cooks." One language outcome could be stated as "The individual reads for critical analysis and evaluation." Outcome statements contain no indicators of the degree of competence the individual exhibits and, therefore, are inadequate on their own for indicating the desired performance. To indicate the degree of competence, we need a statement of the expected quality of the performance, a *standard*.

While the outcome describes what an individual knows, can do, or is like, the standard indicates how well or to what degree the individual knows, can do, or is like the behavior indicated in the outcome. Standards are set by some authority. In the case of educational standards, they are usually set by the school district or the state. Setting standards for graduates requires attaching a statement of expected quality to each desired outcome. The standard for graduation that I propose for the language outcomes is the level of mature proficiency (level 6 on the suggested continuum). When the standard is combined with the outcome statement, a teacher can get a clearer understanding of the expected performance: "The individual reads for critical analysis and evaluation at the level of mature proficiency." To make that standard clear, some specific *criteria* or *performance indicators* based on our observation of individuals regarded as suitable models are needed.

The criteria or performance indicators for language performance are the observable behaviors found in the language use of the standard setters. At every level of performance of an outcome the observable behaviors of the individual will be representative of the behaviors demonstrated by the standard setters. Students writing their first reports on classroom experiences engage in the same behaviors as professional reporters. They organize their information, decide and indicate the relative significance of facts they are presenting, and choose appropriate language for the subject and audience; they draft, revise, and edit their reports. Indicators of the range, flexibility, ability to make connections, control of the conventions, and independence in demonstrating those behaviors make up the criteria for each level because they describe the variations in performance of the outcome across the continuum.

School officials might select level 6 as the graduation standard on the assumption that at graduation from high school it is desirable for individuals to perform habitually at the level demonstrated by educated adults. Describing that standard requires reference to the performance of adults who are functioning successfully in all areas of our complex society. To decide what that standard required I asked myself a number of questions: What language ability in each of the eleven outcomes do adults need in order to successfully perform in responsible jobs? to succeed in continued study at the university level? to be effective parents? to be well-informed voters and political activists? to be contributing members of community organizations (library boards, school boards, church councils, volunteer fire and rescue squads, benevolent societies)? to enjoy and contribute to the artistic life of the community (music, painting, dance, theater, landscaping and gardening, literature)?

Those questions suggest the diverse and complex language demands members of our society face. They also suggest the challenge instructors face in trying to prepare students for full participation in all of these areas. A major goal should be for every graduate to have the language ability to participate in defined zones. Not all graduates will be at the level of mature proficiency on every outcome at graduation. For that reason two levels may be designated, an acceptable level (the level of adult competency) and the benchmark level (the level of mature proficiency). Graduation requirements at the local or state level might be written to require all graduates to have achieved the benchmark level on some outcomes and at least the acceptable level on all.

By benchmark, I mean the level of desired performance for a designated group. Benchmarks in common usage are reference points that describe progress or position. In the present educational context the term is used to mean milestones or targets—the benchmarks are not only reference points but short-term goals. When I suggest that a benchmark for evaluating the progress of any group of learners is level 2, level 4, or level 6 on the continuum, I am suggesting that I hope that all members of the group will be at that level of performance. The points on the continuum (however many have been defined) can all be benchmarks in the sense that they can all serve as reference points to describe performance. However, it is in selecting one point as the benchmark for a particular group that educators can begin to evaluate performance rather than simply to assess it. A teacher assesses performance when she or he says that it falls at level 4 on the continuum; the teacher evaluates performance when she or he says that a particular performance is good. For example, if it is decided that the benchmark for all ninth graders in a school in regard to the outcome of writing for information and understanding is level 4 of this eight-level continuum, teachers can then refer to performance at that level as "good" or some other positive label. Any performance at a lower level is something less than good, perhaps "acceptable," or "fair," or "not yet." Any performance at a higher level is labeled to indicate that it surpasses the benchmark, hence "very good," "excellent," "superior," or "outstanding." A continuum with designated benchmarks can be used to measure elementary, intermediate, and mature performance.

Elementary Performance

Levels 1 through 4 of the eight-level continuum provide a scale for describing early stages of development of an outcome. Level 2 is the target level or benchmark for elementary performance. I am using the term *elementary* in a generic sense rather than as an indication of age or grade. An elementary chess player, for example, is one who is just acquiring the fundamentals of the game. Level 1 indicates performance of the activities (mental or physical) that constitute the outcome but with a very limited range and with considerable reliance on the guidance of a teacher. In the case of the outcome of reading for aesthetic response, the individual's range might be limited to a small number of simple stories, and even within that range the reader would rely on the help of a teacher to understand what is happening in the stories and to make connections with previous literary or life experience. Yet this individual is on the continuum because she can (and does) do what readers do: read and comprehend stories. Remember the crucial distinction made earlier between nonswimmers and beginning swimmers. Once a person can keep afloat and move through the water, that person is on the continuum. Performance might be labeled at level 1 as acceptable for beginners because even though the individual has not reached the benchmark she is showing evidence of beginning to achieve the outcome and is engaged in behaviors representative of experienced performers.

The crucial difference between level 1 performance and the benchmark level, level 2, is that individuals operating at level 1 are dependent on the help of another to carry out the behaviors associated with the task. For each of the four-point scales that can be formed from the eight-point continuum, the first point describes a level of dependent performance that indicates progress toward the benchmark. Level two on the elementary scale indicates independent habitual performance of the behaviors described in the criteria for that benchmark. For example, the criteria for level 2 of the outcome reading for aesthetic response indicate that individuals will read independently a wide range of elementary literature from their own and other cultures and will relate that literature to previous literary and life experiences. The specification of elementary literature distinguishes this level from more advanced levels, and the qualifiers *independently* and *a wide range* distinguish it from the lower level.

The two higher levels on the four-point scale enable us to indicate performance that is exceptionally good. Level 3 refers to performance beyond the elementary benchmark and indicative of dependent intermediate performance. In any group of learners some learners will move rapidly through the elementary level on at least some outcomes and begin to work at the activities of more experienced learners. Level-3 readers for information, for example, will be reading young adult texts or simple general-interest materials with the help of a teacher to find information, while the other learners in their group are still using simple elementary material for the same purpose. Level-4 readers in this group read a wider range of young adult texts and general-interest material to find information *and* do so independently.

This four-point scale can be used to assess the progress of any group of beginning learners and describe their performance relative to the benchmark. Whether educators want to report the progress of fourth graders for the purposes of statewide assessment or indicate the progress of a group of adult literacy students, this same scale can be used. For each of the assessed outcomes, almost certainly some students will be performing at level 1, a number at the level-2 benchmark, some who have already moved ahead to level 3, and a few who are already at level 4, which is the benchmark for intermediate performance. Evaluative labels for those levels might be the same ones used for the adult levels above: "acceptable," "good," "very good," and "outstanding." These labels indicate the strength of the performance relative to the benchmark for that group of learners. Because in a school setting instructors are always working on many outcomes at the same time, it is important to recognize that students will be good or very good on some outcomes while they are just acceptable on others.

Intermediate Performance

The intermediate scale is the middle four points—levels 3 through 6—of the eight-point continuum. For this scale the benchmark is level 4, the independent intermediate level. At level 3 the learners are engaged in the activities described in the criteria for the intermediate level but, as in the case of level 1, their range of activities is limited and they are dependent on the guidance of a teacher. The range of material for level-3 reading for information and understanding includes young adult texts (especially school textbooks) and simple general-interest materials (popular magazines, local newspapers, and reference materials such as dictionaries and atlases). In a school situation this would mean that these learners would be able to read the textbooks used in the high school classes, understand information presented there and would also be able to use some general reference materials. The learners at level 4 would use similar materials to obtain information, but their range would be greater, especially in the types of general reference materials that they could use, and they could obtain and interpret information from these sources without the help of a teacher.

The level-5 learners demonstrate the criteria for adult minimal competency. Performance at that level, as at levels 1 and 3, depends on assistance from a more experienced person or from printed models or directions. That performance would be considered very good for the group for whom the benchmark is level 4, and the habitual performance that defines the criteria for level 6—the level of mature adult proficiency—would be considered outstanding.

In a school situation this intermediate scale would likely be used to assess the performance of students who are ready to enter senior high school. Level 4, the benchmark for this group, indicates that learners are ready to function independently on the types of reading, writing, and oral language tasks and with the type of material that is required for high school study. Students at level 3 on an outcome will need considerable assistance from teachers and peers to succeed in high school study. Those below level 3 will need modified materials (such as less-complex textbooks) and a great deal of teacher assistance to succeed. On the other hand, students who are already at level 5 on an outcome need opportunities to perform the activities defined for that level (reading more complex material, writing in more sophisticated forms) with the help of a teacher and with many models to follow. Students at level 6 will need opportunities to range on their own beyond the material and tasks required for the course and to seek out and try increasingly challenging activities.

Mature Performance

The purpose of standard setting and outcomes-based education is to insure that at graduation all students will demonstrate acceptable habitual performance for each desired learning outcome. The benchmark for adult performance of the outcomes is level 6, by definition, the level of independent mature proficiency. I have tried to describe that level for the language outcomes according to what seem to be real world demands for adults to participate in every area of society. For each of the desired outcomes, educators will have to decide what criteria designate the performance of fully functioning mature adults in our society, recognizing that as society and its demands change so will the criteria for that level. As stated above, not every student will achieve the benchmark level of mature proficiency on every outcome by graduation. On some outcomes some individuals will be performing at level 5, the level of minimum adult competency. Like the other dependent levels, it suggests performance that is still developing and that relies on the guidance and direction of others. I doubt that instructors would ever want to settle for minimum competency as the final level of habitual performance for any individual, but some may consider it acceptable because such performance is sufficiently developed to indicate that with continued practice the individual will improve to meet the demands of society.

Level 7 indicates adult performance that is exceptionally good and calls attention to itself by its excellence. Some high school seniors already demonstrate achievement of some outcomes to such an exceptional degree. There are even some graduating seniors who already have demonstrated unique talent and achievement in some outcomes that indicates they are in the class of professional standard setters, level 8. That sounds unlikely when extremely high standards associated with professional performance are considered. Yet in every area of human endeavor performers are recognized who at a very early age distinguish themselves as champions. Such performance is taken rather lightly in some areas: musical prodigies, superior child athletes, teenage grandmasters of chess. In academic areas there are also occasional geniuses who perform at the highest level on some outcomes.

Although the two levels of exceptional and standard-setting performance are far beyond the competency of most high school seniors, I think that there is great value in keeping these two levels in mind in student assessment. They remind teachers and students that there is no ceiling to excellent performance. Students who at an early age reach the benchmark required for graduation have the advantage of being able to use the rest of their high school days to pursue more challenging experiences in that area to allow them to develop to the fullest extent possible.

There will be standards. We must encourage our students to set them.

Individuals and Standards

Any discussion of setting or raising educational standards is sure to include the issues of equity and excellence. These twin goals are often seen to be in conflict. Many people concerned with encouraging excellence fear that by setting standards that can be achieved by all learners, the incentive for some learners to excel will be removed. I believe that the most important safeguard against such leveling of expectations is the mindfulness of a continuum that includes the top levels of performance. Educators should never set a ceiling for the performance of students or even fix their sights so firmly on a particular benchmark that the possibilities beyond cannot be seen. The presence of professional standards is certain to encourage some students to work toward that standard on those outcomes for which they have special talent. Students who discover they have talent for writing poetry will strive to match the achievement of professional poets as surely as the gifted basketball player tries to equal Michael Jordan.

Another equally important measure for insuring excellence is the provision of a variety of ways for individuals to achieve the common outcomes. If outcomes are to be achieved by all students they must be broad enough to allow for a great diversity of performance. The descriptions of the language outcomes suggest something of that diversity. Listed in the category of outstanding writers for aesthetic expression are writers of poetry, novels, children's picture books, and screenplays, and in the category of readers for information and understanding scholars of every discipline and profession are to be found. There are as many routes to becoming an outstanding language user as there are talented people to pursue them, which is an important factor to keep in mind when critics concerned with equity express their fear that common standards mean that the hurdles will be raised even higher for students who are already having difficulty achieving success. If all students are to be successful in an outcomes-based program, educators will have to establish equally challenging and significant hurdles in many different disciplines and areas of interest in order to provide opportunities for students to achieve the desired learning outcomes through the investigation of areas that match student interests, talents, and ambitions. Outcomes that allow for diverse paths to attainment may provide for real equity without insisting on uniformity.

Outcomes Assessment

The descriptions of the continuum and the benchmarks suggest a process for assessing and evaluating the performance of individuals on the desired learning outcomes. The kind of criteria identified for the language outcomes and the characteristics of habitual performance of an outcome can't be assessed on the basis of individual tests or experiences. Such assessment requires, as James Moffett (1970) recommended, synthesizing "the totality of observations—from different times and vantage points—into a fuller picture." Capturing that fuller picture will mean setting aside many traditional notions of who makes decisions about student performance and how those decisions are made.

In traditional grading, teachers are responsible for assigning a grade to each student. Teachers take the task of grading very seriously. When I began investigating the concept of language outcomes, I started by asking a great number of English teachers, "What does a grade in your class mean?" Invariably the teachers could tell me with absolute precision how they computed grades. Some had simple systems of figuring arithmetic averages by adding all grades in the grade book and dividing by the number of entries. Others had very sophisticated calculations that weighted some classroom activities more heavily than others, subtracted for lateness, and gave extra credit for special projects. Without exception, the teachers knew their grading system perfectly and had great confidence in its fairness and reliability. But none of them could answer with confidence my question about what the grade meant. And all of them were quick to admit that their grades probably did not mean the same thing as those of any other teacher in the school, even if that other teacher taught the same course.

The diversity of teacher grading systems is unlikely to change as schools switch to outcomes-based programs. There may be more agreement on the expectations for a course when teachers begin to work together toward the same outcomes, but different grading systems based on the individual teacher's values will undoubtedly remain. In addition to the course grades that individual teachers have responsibility for, however, there will also be outcomes assessment that all teachers will contribute to. This assessment will differ from grading in that it will focus on the habitual performance of desired learning outcomes that transcend the particular demands of any one course. For effective assessment of the outcomes, instructors will need a system that depends on multiple sources of information and multiple judges. A system that includes the professional judgments of the local educators, supported by a portfolio of student work and validated by external tests (district, state, or national) offers the greatest possibility of getting the full picture.

Professional Judgment and Student Profiles

Assessing student achievement of desired learning outcomes should be neither individual nor idiosyncratic. Educators must have a variety of viewers and viewpoints to get the fuller picture. The best way of getting those viewpoints is to allow every professional in the school who works with a student to have a say in assessing the performance of that student. There may be some outcomes that only a limited number of specialists in the school are capable of assessing, but certainly for language outcomes the observations of all of the student's teachers, coaches, and counselors will bring teachers closer to the truth of the student's habitual performance. The diversity of the experiences in each curricular and extracurricular area combined with the different attitude and aptitude the student brings to those experiences guarantees that individual observers will have different perceptions of that student's language proficiency. When professionals in the school agree on the criteria for the desired outcomes, they can contribute knowledgeably to the assessment of the language performance of all the students they know.

The collective professional judgment of the school faculty is the most important element in an assessment system. That judgment can be reported in a student profile listing all the outcomes with a four-point scale referenced to the continuum above. Figure 4-2 presents two profiles from which to choose for reporting attainment of language outcomes. Profile A groups the outcomes according to function categories. Profile B groups them according to the domains of reading, writing, and listening and speaking. Both profiles give a sense of the individual's strengths and weaknesses as a language user and her preferred modes.

Figure 4-2a

Student Language Profile by Function

	Acceptable	Good	Very Good	Outstanding
Personal Response & Expression:				
Listening/Speaking	1	2	3	4
Reading	1	2	3	4
Writing	1	2	3	4
Information & Understanding:				
Listening/speaking	1	2	3	4
Reading	1	2	3	4
Writing	1	2	3	4
Critical Analysis & Evaluation:				
Listening/Speaking	1	2	3	4
Reading	1	2	3	4
Writing	1	2	3	4

Profiles for graduating students or students at the end of the elementary or middle grades can be completed by asking every professional (teachers, counselors, coaches, librarians) in the building to rate those students on any outcomes they have had significant opportunity to observe. All raters would have copies of the outcomes continua with criteria for each of the four levels. Guidance counselors and/or senior teachers might each have responsibility for completing the profile for a number of seniors with input from all the raters. Those teachers would not only record the collective judgment of the school professionals on the students' performance on each outcome but would also be responsible for reconciling differences in judgments.

Procedures for assembling the profile and reaching consensus among the professionals who know the student may be difficult at first. With time and experience teachers will have criteria for the levels of performance in mind as they work with students and will respond as readily to a question about the level of student performance in listening and speaking for information, for example, as they do now when asked how well a student can spell or punctuate. As

Figure 4-2b
Student Language Profile by Domain

	Acceptable	Good	Very Good	Outstanding
Listening/Speaking for:				
Personal Response	1	2	3	4
Social Interaction	1	2	3	4
Information & Understanding	1	2	3	4
Critical Analysis & Evaluation	1	2	3	4
Reading for:				
Personal Response	1	2	3	4
Information & Understanding	1	2	3	4
Critical Analysis & Evaluation	1	2	3	4
Writing for:				
Personal Expression	1	2	3	4
Social Interaction	1	2	3	4
Information & Understanding	1	2	3	4
Critical Analysis & Evaluation	1	2	3	4

the outcomes and criteria become more familiar to the entire school community, students and their parents and teachers will be consciously working together to help students achieve the outcomes and will be discussing student progress in the outcomes on an ongoing basis. In that situation, the completed profile will not contain information new or surprising to students or their parents but will be a public record of information they have agreed on.

Portfolios

The term *portfolio* is used to mean a wide variety of related but distinct practices. The exact nature, content, and procedures for portfolios are determined by the purpose for which they are being used. For large-scale assessment of outcomes, a major purpose of portfolios is likely to be accountability. Portfolios provide supporting evidence for judgments the local professionals make about students' level of outcomes attainment, a use of portfolios that differs from the integration of portfolios as a regular part of classroom practice in a number of ways. Whereas the portfolio might be used in the classroom as the basis of a grade (that is, the portfolio is evaluated), in outcomes assessment the portfolio is the evidence that supports the evaluation (that is, habitual performance is being evaluated). Portfolios used as the basis for class grades most often include the "best pieces" of student work. Portfolios used to support outcomes assessment include typical pieces that reflect the habitual performance of the individual as well as some pieces that show the limits of the individual's range. The latter pieces may be less well formed than other work that the individual has accomplished because these pieces represent new levels of challenge for this learner. It is also quite likely that for outcomes assessment teachers and students will have less latitude in assembling portfolios because of the need to include pieces that reflect the public criteria for the outcomes. In the classroom students and teacher together decide on the criteria as well as select the pieces.

In assembling a portfolio to reflect the level of an individual's attainment of the desired outcomes, it is not necessary to include a piece for each outcome. Representative sampling will probably suffice for accountability, and one piece may reflect performance on several outcomes; for example, a research paper on a historical topic may provide evidence of the student's ability to read and write for information and understanding as well as an understanding of political, economic, and social issues in global society (a possible outcome related to social studies). Similarly, a tape of a student's participation in a debate on garbage incinerators reveals an ability to listen, speak, and read for critical analysis and evaluation as well as the ability to analyze and evaluate problems and issues related to the natural world (a possible science outcome). Although the portfolio need not contain evidence of each outcome, I think that it should contain evidence of each category of outcome: aesthetic, social, informational, and critical. For each category student work could come from any curriculum area, thereby providing evidence of a considerable range of learning within relatively few pieces and providing opportunity for the student to demonstrate language proficiency through achievements in areas of personal interest.

The most beneficial aspect of portfolios, according to the teachers who use them, is the involvement of the students in reflective self-assessment. Students learn through their involvement in setting up portfolio procedures, in selecting samples of their own work that reflect the criteria and present the best evidence of their competence, and in reentering the portfolio regularly to revise its contents to reflect new levels of performance. Dennie Palmer Wolf's work in portfolios makes it clear that portfolios are more than a new technology for assessment. The process of collecting, revising, and interpreting the contents of the portfolios creates a culture in the classroom that involves students and teachers in "intense discussion of standards and evidence," that helps students to become "competent assessors of their own work" through "sustained opportunities to internalize standards and ways of questioning and improving the quality of their work" (Wolf et al. 1991, 59).

External Tests

At least for the short term, large-scale formal testing will continue to assure the public of the quality of local academic programs and the validity of the school's assessments. The strength of the national standards movement is evidence of public pressure for external measures of school achievement. Formal tests produced by state agencies, national projects, or commercial testing services provide common measures providing assurances of the comparability of the learning in diverse schools.

Teachers have always felt some resentment toward external tests: tests impinge on the amount of time available for teacher-devised activities; they provide only partial pictures of students' abilities and achievements; they fragment learning; they are artificial situations; they are biased; they produce undue anxiety in students; and they result in some students being labeled as deficient. Much of the resentment toward tests, however, derives not from tests and their limitations (which are admittedly numerous) but from the disproportionate weight often given to these tests when making decisions about students. Because test results are often reported in newspapers, and used to determine student eligibility for graduation or promotion and evaluate teacher effectiveness, some tests acquire a significance many educators believe is inappropriate.

At the same time that there is pressure for accountability and common standards, the use of traditional tests in such a public way and for "high stakes" purposes has come under criticism from educators and from policymakers. Assessment reforms in individual states such as California, Connecticut, New York, and Vermont, as well as national efforts such as the Council of Chief State School Officers Assessment Consortium and the New Standards project, are aimed at the development of an assessment system in which external tests constitute only one part of a comprehensive assessment that is a combination of external tests and teacher judgments. In such a system, tests may take on less importance as public attention is directed to more authentic assessment measures in the form of projects, exhibitions, and graduation portfolios. As these authentic measures gain credibility, it may be that results on external tests will be reported in the form of a distribution of scores, rather than by individual students, and will be used mainly for program evaluation and validation of local assessment practice.

Outcomes Assessment and Classroom Assessment

Outcomes assessment can provide a valuable service to the student, the school, and the community by insuring that all students achieve the standards of excellence. The assessment of outcomes achievement, however, is not sufficient to provide all the information wanted about the content and quality of student learning. Employers and colleges will continue to be interested in what students studied in school, how well they performed in their chosen areas of study, and what curricular and cocurricular experiences they have had. Student records and transcripts will continue to include lists of courses taken and successfully completed, grades attained in those courses, and school clubs and activities in which the student participated, in addition to the profile of the student's proficiency on the desired learning outcomes.

Outcomes assessment may serve best as a general "taking stock" at major passages in the student's school career, perhaps at the end of elementary, middle, and high school or at specific grades such as four, eight, and twelve as suggested by the national standards movement. On the other hand, classroom assessment is ongoing, focused on specific requirements of a course or grade level, and as formal or informal as the local school requires. The two types of assessment, though, are intricately related. First, the substance of the outcomes assessment comes out of regular curricular and cocurricular activities. Teachers form their judgments on students' habitual demonstration of an outcome based on the numerous and diverse experiences of the school program. The samples of student work included in the portfolio are papers, projects, or exhibitions completed in regular classes or cocurricular activities. Second, the two types of assessment are linked because the curriculum is intentionally designed to insure that students achieve the outcomes. Teachers do not have to decide after the fact whether work students did in their class will be useful in providing examples of performance of the outcomes. Class experiences in an outcomes-based program are planned to require such performances, and performance standards for the outcomes are always kept in mind by teachers and students.

The major difference between the two types of assessment is that regular classroom assessment focuses on individual demonstrations of learning rather than on overall habitual performance. For example, in writing assessment teaches give grades based on the quality of individual pieces according to agreed upon criteria for the task. Instructors may grade a critical essay based on factors related to the rhetorical task, organization, style and voice, and conventions. The *product* is being evaluated. At the end of a semester the student's grade in writing may be the average of grades received on a number of products, such as pieces of writing. If those pieces of writing are of good quality, the student receives a good grade for the course. But, at the same time, the teacher might recognize while assessing the *range* of topics, the student's *flexibility* in using different forms and addressing different audiences for different purposes, and the facility for suiting *conventions* to purpose and audience that the student hasn't yet achieved the desired level of performance for the writing outcomes. The student might pass the course but still require more experience and help to achieve the outcome standard.

The traditional distinction of formative and summative evaluation is relevant in distinguishing classroom assessment from outcomes assessment. Classroom assessment is primarily formative and focuses on guiding the individual's progress; it seeks to reward incremental gains and to compare today's performance to yesterday's. In order to encourage and direct student efforts, teachers provide regular feedback, whether in the form of evaluative comments or formal grades, for daily activities and performances. Report cards are most useful for indicating the progress the student is making in doing the activities valued in the classroom. The recent trend toward narrative reports enables teachers to describe student growth since the last report with respect to standards for the class, and instructors can describe what the student is doing and indicate new challenges the student will be undertaking in the next semester. These narratives provide opportunities for parents as well as teachers to keep track of student development and to make some decisions about how to help students to continue to make progress. A narrative report also can provide an opportunity to indicate how progress in meeting the expectations of the class is contributing to the student's achievement of the desired learning outcomes. For example, one comment on a narrative report might read, "William is beginning to use general reference materials in the library to locate information for his reports. This is one of the criteria for students in the middle school for the outcome for reading for information."

If a school does not use a narrative report but uses traditional report cards with letter or number grades for each subject, the teacher can provide other information to parents to indicate what the grade represents and how it is determined. Such material might be sent as an enclosure in the report card, or it might be presented to parents in an individual conference or group meeting. It is important if grades continue to be used that everyone know what they mean with regard to the expectations of the course as well as in relation to the student's progress toward the desired learning outcomes. Information included in the reports to parents might answer these or similar questions:

What are the goals of this course for the student?
How do the activities of the course relate to attainment of those goals?
What are the criteria for satisfactory performance in the course?
How satisfactorily is the student meeting the goals and objectives of the course?
What could the student do to improve performance in the course?
How do the activities of the course relate to attainment of desired learning outcomes?
What evidence is there of the student's progress toward achievement of the outcomes?

Answers to such questions are necessary for students and parents to understand and participate in planning educational programs. The answers to these questions, especially about the relationship of classroom activities and assessment to the development of desired learning outcomes, are also of great interest to other educators. To insure consistency of educational outcomes and standards in classrooms and schools across the nation, the experience and expertise of outstanding teachers must inform the process of setting and applying those standards. The next chapter reports on a pilot study of outcomes assessment in which some outstanding high school teachers used the outcomes continua described in this book to assess the language use of some of their students and to begin to address some questions about the relationship of outcomes to classroom practice.

Summary

Definitions

- *Outcomes:* The knowledge, skills, and understandings that individuals can and do habitually demonstrate as a result of instruction and experience.
- *Standards:* Statement of the level of performance expected by some authority.
- *Criteria or Performance Indicators:* Observable behaviors that give evidence of the level of performance.

- *Levels:* Clearly defined positions on a continuum of performance.
- *Continuum:* Description of an identifiable performance (outcome) as it progresses with reference to some variable factors (such as range, flexibility, connections, conventions, and independence) from rudimentary to standard setting.
- *Benchmark:* A reference point for assessing performance. A level on the continuum can be identified as the benchmark for assessing the performance of a group of students.

Characteristics of Outcomes Assessment

- *Criterion Based:* Agreed-upon public criteria for designated levels of performance that are based on the behavior of standard-setting professionals.
- *Milestones:* Formal assessment and reporting of outcomes achievement takes place at significant turning-points of students' schooling (such as at the end of elementary, middle, and high schools).
- *Foundational:* Clear connections between outcomes and all other aspects of the school program.
- *System:* Three-part system of assessment:

  1. Student profile reflecting the professional judgment of local educators

  2. Student portfolio containing samples of work that give evidence to support the evaluation

  3. External tests that insure consistency of standards across schools and validate local assessments

Chapter Five

A Pilot Study of Language Outcomes

In 1989 members of the Bureau of English Language Arts at the State Education Department in New York in consultation with a number of teachers developed a draft of language outcomes and continua. A group of those teachers agreed to conduct a pilot study using the outcomes in their classrooms to assess the language proficiency of some of their students and to report their findings back to me at the State Education Department. That study provided valuable information to us at the State Education Department to begin revising the outcomes themselves and develop a process of outcomes-based assessment in the area of English language arts. The most important insights and discoveries of the individual teachers can only be explained by the teachers themselves, and I will not presume here to try to tell their stories for them. Some of them have presented their experiences at professional conferences and workshops, and their experiences are useful to other educators who are trying to implement a program of outcomes-based education.

However, the collective reports of the teachers who completed the study have been useful to the Bureau in revising and expanding the draft to produce the version of outcomes that appears in the Appendix. The collective reports may also be useful to school district curriculum developers responsible for setting and assessing standards students must achieve and for planning instructional programs. In this chapter I present the reports with the observations of the teachers in the study and some reviewers with a minimum of interpretive comment. At the end of this chapter I raise some questions based on this study that could help set a direction for future implementation of outcomes-based assessment. I first describe the study itself.

Procedures for the Pilot Study

Each teacher in the study selected three students to follow. In most cases the students were seniors, but some juniors and even sophomores were included. I asked the teachers to select students who represent different levels of academic achievement: one of their best students, one middle-of-the-road student, and one struggling student. Because the teachers were all from different types of schools with different teaching assignments, I expected that this process would provide a wide range of ability in the sample and give the teachers a chance to analyze factors that distinguish levels of performance among their students.

The teachers spent some time during the first semester of the school year familiarizing themselves with the outcomes and the performance indicators for the four levels of adult performance. A definition of outcomes and a brief description of the levels and the characteristics of performance were provided to establish a common understanding. Teachers were invited to consult with each other, me, and other members of the Bureau during the study. It was clear in the narratives and teacher reflections on the project that the amount of involvement teachers had in the development of the outcomes—and the amount of conversation we had as they worked with the outcomes in class—proved to be a significant factor in the extent to which they internalized the standards and displayed confidence in making judgments about student performance. Our conversations helped us all to come to a common understanding of what it could mean to consider student performance in relation to the standards set by outstanding adult readers, writers, and speakers rather than in comparison with other students. It required a major shift in thinking for all of us.

During the spring semester the teachers observed performance in each of the eleven language outcomes of the three students they had selected. They collected evidence of "habitual" demonstration in each of those outcomes. At the end of the semester they sent in reports that contained:

1. A language profile for each student with designations of the level of habitual performance for each outcome (See Figure 5-1).

Figure 5-1
Student Language Profile

	Acceptable	Good	Very Good	Outstanding
Listening/Speaking for:				
Personal Response	1	2	3	4
Social Interaction	1	2	3	4
Information & Understanding	1	2	3	4
Critical Analysis & Evaluation	1	2	3	4
Reading for:				
Personal Response	1	2	3	4
Information & Understanding	1	2	3	4
Critical Analysis & Evaluation	1	2	3	4
Writing for:				
Personal Expression	1	2	3	4
Social Interaction	1	2	3	4
Information & Understanding	1	2	3	4
Critical Analysis & Evaluation	1	2	3	4

2. A portfolio for each student to support the teacher's judgment. The portfolio was to contain only three samples, one for each of the language domains (reading, writing, and listening/speaking). The sample for each domain was to be for the language function in which the student was most proficient. For example, if the teacher judged the student to be more proficient at reading for information and understanding than for aesthetic response or critical analysis, the teacher would include a sample of the student's work in informational reading. All the samples in the portfolio were written products, whether the outcomes being assessed were in writing, reading, or listening/speaking. For listening/speaking a student reflection on an oral language performance was included. For reading a written response to a reading was included.

3. A brief narrative by the teacher describing the habitual performance of the student in each outcome.

4. A reflection on the process by the teacher. The reflection included any problems or concerns about the process of outcomes assessment, suggestions for revising the outcomes, recommendations for designing the portfolio for large-scale assessment, and responses to some key questions.

The Language Profiles

A review of the language profiles returned by the teachers yielded a number of interesting observations and questions. Figure 5-2 provides a summary of the student rankings on a function dominant profile. The number in each column indicates the aggregate number of students in the study who performed at that level according to the

Figure 5-2
Summary of Student Rankings by Function

	Acceptable	Good	Very Good	Outstanding
Personal Response & Expression:				
Listening/Speaking	1 = 6	2 = 7	3 = 11	4 = 3
Reading	1 = 6	2 = 5	3 = 10	4 = 6
Writing	1 = 8	2 = 7	3 = 8	4 = 4
Information & Understanding:				
Listening/speaking	NA = 1 1 = 6	2 = 7	3 = 10	4 = 3
Reading	1 = 7	2 = 7	3 = 9	4 = 4
Writing	1 = 7	2 = 10	3 = 6	4 = 4
Critical Analysis & Evaluation:				
Listening/Speaking	NA = 1 1 = 7	2 = 9	3 = 9	4 = 1
Reading	1 = 9	2 = 7	3 = 8	4 = 3
Writing	1 = 10	2 = 6	3 = 9	4 = 2
Social Interaction				
Listening/Speaking	1 = 5	2 = 8	3 = 13	4 = 1
Writing	NA = 3 1 = 8	2 = 9	3 = 6	4 = 1

N = 27

Figure 5-3

Summary of Student Rankings by Domain

	Acceptable	Good	Very Good	Outstanding
Listening/Speaking for:				
Personal Response	1 = 6	2 = 7	3 = 11	4 = 3
Social Interaction	1 = 5	2 = 8	3 = 13	4 = 1
Information & Understanding	NA = 1 1 = 6	2 = 7	3 = 10	4 = 3
Critical Analysis & Evaluation	NA = 1 1 = 7	2 = 9	3 = 9	4 = 1
Reading for:				
Personal Response	1 = 6	2 = 5	3 = 10	4 = 6
Information & Understanding	1 = 7	2 = 7	3 = 9	4 = 4
Critical Analysis & Evaluation	1 = 9	2 = 7	3 = 8	4 = 3
Writing for:				
Personal Expression	1 = 8	2 = 7	3 = 8	4 = 4
Social Interaction	NA = 1 1 = 8	2 = 9	3 = 6	4 = 1
Information & Understanding	1 = 7	2 = 10	3 = 6	4 = 4
Critical Analysis & Evaluation	1 = 10	2 = 6	3 = 9	4 = 2

judgment of the teachers. Figure 5-3 contains the same information presented on a domain dominant profile.

As those summaries show, the students in the study were rated generally quite high. Based on the definitions of the levels, I had expected that habitual performance of graduating seniors would be at either level 5 or 6 in most cases with only a few exceptional instances of performance at level 7 or 8. As you can see from the summary profiles, the ratings did not fall that way. The only outcomes for which the highest numbers of students were at level 6, the level of mature adult proficiency, were writing for information and understanding and listening and speaking for critical analysis and evaluation. On eight of the outcomes the largest number of students were at the seventh level, the level of exceptional adult proficiency. Far fewer students were rated at the eighth level, the standard-setting professional level, for any of the outcomes than at any other level, but there were still many more at that level than I had expected based on its definition as standard-setting performance.

A number of factors might account for the high ratings. Far from being a scientifically controlled research sample, the group was made up of twenty-seven purposely selected students from the classes of ten exceptionally fine English teachers. Some of the teachers in the study taught only college-bound students, and all of the teachers purposely selected one of their very best students to follow. Therefore, there were a large number of high-performing students in the group. There may also be a tendency for teachers to rate the performance of their own students as above average even though they are less positive in their estimation of student performance in general, a finding similar to that of recent studies indicating that Americans tend to think their local schools are performing well even though they think American schools in general are less than satisfactory. Another possible explanation of this distribution of ratings may be the difficulty teachers have making what is referred to as a "paradigm shift." Accustomed to arraying student performance on a scale from fair to excellent or from D to A with reference to the performance of other students, the teachers probably tended to make the same distribution on the outcomes continua in spite of the criteria. It is a significant change to compare the performance of high school students with the standards set by professional writers, readers, and speakers rather than a relative ranking with other high school students.

The tendency to put a number of students in the highest levels of proficiency suggest that it might be desirable to construct a continuum in such a way that teachers can make distinctions about the degree of proficiency within the broad levels of performance. Some reviewers suggested a continuum with fewer levels for student performance (elementary, intermediate, and commencement) but with three possible degrees of attainment of each of those levels (perhaps called "dependent," "proficient," and "superior"). Such a scale would allow teachers to indicate finer distinctions among student performance without lowering standards for higher levels. It would also counteract a tendency to push young students to read or write material that may not be as valuable for their stage of development in order to challenge more capable students. With designations of degree of attainment, a teacher could account for the performance of an exceptionally accomplished graduating senior as superior performance at the commencement level. Modification of the continuum to incorporate this thinking is one possibility for designing an outcomes-based assessment most useful to teachers. Even with that modification, there is value in keeping the two levels of exceptional and standard-setting performance on the continuum to make it clear that all levels of performance are defined with reference to those standard setters and to provide for recognition of the occasional student prodigies.

Another interesting aspect of the profiles is evident when looking at the charts of individual student profiles (Figure 5-4). A major advantage of the language profile for assessing students' language abilities is the possibility of indicating different areas of strength and weakness. In some of the profiles relative strengths and weaknesses are apparent, but in a few cases individuals are rated at the same level in all language outcomes. That finding also supported the need for indicators of degrees of attainment within the broad levels.

In some cases teachers indicated they did not have enough evidence to evaluate a student's performance of a particular language outcome. Several students didn't receive ratings for listening/speaking for at least one outcome. Teacher narratives commented on the lack of opportunity for observing students' habitual performance as listeners and speakers or the lack of specific instances of oral language performance to support their general sense of student proficiency. One teacher commented on the difficulty of assessing listening and speaking together and suggested that when she thought about the skills involved she wanted to pair the language domains as reading and listening and as writing and speaking. Following the same line of thinking, another teacher speculated that an evaluator might assume from one student's academic achievement that she must be an effective listener since so much instruction in the high school comes through teacher lecture, but at the same time a teacher might have little or conflicting evidence of the same student's ability as a speaker, making it difficult to decide on one level of performance. Another problem for some teachers in assessing listening/ speaking was that the function categories seemed less discrete in oral language situations than in reading and writing. A few teachers indicated a level of performance for listening/speaking in general rather than by function. A blurring of categories was also apparent in the samples that were included in the portfolios, confirming the belief of all of us in the project that the categories are not discrete even though they may be convenient for describing various elements of student language use. In some cases the teachers indicated they did not have enough evidence to describe those elements separately; in other cases, separating out elements that were so closely mingled in practice seemed artificial.

Figure 5-4
Charts of Individual Student Profiles

PF

	A	S	I	C		A	S	I	C		A	S	I	C
	Ellen					**Vicky**					**Joe**			
L/S	3	3	3	2		3	3	2	2		2	1	1	1
R	3		3	2		3		2	2		2		1	1
W	3	3	2	3		2	2	1	2		1	1	2	1

C & C

	A	S	I	C		A	S	I	C		A	S	I	C
	Cecelia					**Larry**					**Jamie**			
L/S	1	1	1	1		2	2	3	2		4	3	4	4
R	1		1	1		3		2	3		4		4	4
W	1	1	1	1		2	2	2	2		4	4	4	4

JQ

	A	S	I	C		A	S	I	C		A	S	I	C
	Joan					**Gil**					**Burke**			
L/S	3	3	3	3		3	3	3	3		4	4	4	3
R	3		3	3		3		3	2		4		4	4
W	3	3	3	3		3	2	3	2		4	3	4	3

RT

	A	S	I	C		A	S	I	C		A	S	I	C
	Maura					**Randall**					**Chris**			
L/S	1	2	1	2		3	3	2	2		2	2	3	3
R	1		1	1		2		2	2		3		3	3
W	1	1	2	1		2	2	2	2		4	3	4	3

NZ

	A	S	I	C		A	S	I	C		A	S	I	C
	Johanna					**Carl**					**Frank**			
L/S	3	2	3	3		2	3	3	2		3	3	4	3
R	4		3	3		1		3	3		4		4	3
W	3	3	4	4		1	1	3	3		2	2	1	1

PK

	A	S	I	C		A	S	I	C		A	S	I	C
	Arthur					**Kenneth**					**Therese**			
L/S	4	3	3	3		3	2	2	1		2	3	2	2
R	3		2	2		2		2	1		2		2	2
W	4	2	2	2		2	2	2	1		2	2	2	2

Figure 5-4
(continued)

Teacher		A S I C	A S I C	A S I C
PH-Z		Sam	Janet	Cindy
	L/S	1 1 1 1	1 2 1	3 3 2 2
	R	2 1 1	1 1 1	4 3 3
	W	1 1 1 1	1 1 1 1	3 3 2 3
GB		Jerry	Donna	Leah
	L/S	1 1 1 1	1 1 1 1	3 3 3 3
	R	1 1 1	1 1 1	4 3 3
	W	1 1 1 1	1 1 1 1	2 2 3 3
(KS)		Gina	Lorraine	Keith
	L/S	3 2 3 3	2 3 2	2 2 2 2
	R	3 4 4	3 3 2	3 2 1
	W	3 3 3	3 3 3	3 2 1

Portfolios

The writing samples in the portfolios reveal how integrally related the functions of language are in practice and provide evidence of the teacher's understanding of the kind of language use that reflects those functions. The samples show the wide variation one would expect. Some teachers labeled the samples with the outcome each one represented or indicated the outcome in the accompanying narrative, but some samples were included without identifying comment. In those cases it was sometimes not obvious which outcome the piece was meant to indicate, suggesting a blurring of functions in actual practice. Few pieces of writing belonged exclusively to one function category (aesthetic, informational, critical, or social); in most pieces students moved in and out of those categories as the focus of their thinking shifted slightly. Pieces that were predominantly critical contained passages of explication of relevant information, and aesthetic pieces often contained critical analysis and evaluative comments. Therefore, the sample one teacher included to provide evidence of a student's ability to present a written critical analysis might be very similar in form and content to a sample included by another teacher to indicate a student's ability to convey information clearly and coherently.

In the case of the outcomes for reading in all three functions, the samples included in the portfolio necessarily provided evidence of more than one outcome since all of the samples were written. Several teachers commented on the impossibility of assessing reading proficiency apart from the ability to explain through written or oral presentation the meaning being made from the text. Therefore, the samples included in the portfolio to indicate student reading abilities also provided evidence of writing abilities. However, the pieces included in the portfolio do contain evidence of the kind of thinking about texts described in the performance indicators for the reading outcomes, making them valuable for supporting teachers' judgments about student reading performance. Their usefulness for indicating writing achievement is an additional value.

As one might expect, written samples are less valuable for indicating performance of the listening/speaking outcomes. Teacher evaluations and student reflections are useful explanations of student performance on listening/speaking outcomes, but they don't provide direct evidence for an external reviewer to confirm those evaluations. Written samples provide some evidence of students' ability to listen and to explain meaning they find in orally presented material but not of speaking abilities. For that purpose portfolios might include audio or video tapes of actual oral language situations, a procedure that was not feasible for the pilot study but might be considered for actual implementation of a similar assessment system.

The total collection of samples of student work from all the teachers provided a rich array of evidence of the wide range of language experiences students engage in as part of their school programs. These collected samples indicate the complexity of the real language performances of students and the impossibility and undesirability of looking at the outcomes as discrete and separable. The samples also suggest the differing expectations of teachers for student performance in language.

In looking at samples of work, it is important to remember that while a profile indicates habitual performance, the pieces in the portfolio are individual instances of performance. Even if those pieces are typical, they are limited in what they reveal. A much more extensive collection is needed to provide a full picture of student range, flexibility, ability to make connections, control of conventions, and independence. The logistics and desirability of putting together such a portfolio still need to be determined.

Teacher Narratives

The teacher narratives were invaluable in reviewing the pilot study, which is both good news and bad news. The utility of the narratives is good news for three reasons. First, the narratives provide insights into student performance that profiles and portfolios alone do not. Second, the narratives help guide the revision of both the outcomes and the process of outcomes assessment. And finally, narratives give models and directions for other teachers implementing outcomes assessment. But the usefulness of narratives is bad news because as researchers the teachers and I had hoped that the other elements of outcomes assessment would be sufficient and that the narratives wouldn't be needed after the pilot study.

One consideration in asking each teacher in the study to follow only three students was the amount of time required to write narratives for each student for each outcome. With eleven outcomes for each of three students, every teacher wrote up to thirty-three brief narratives. The teachers in the study acknowledged the time-consuming nature of this task, and many questioned whether they could have completed the project if they were following more students. At the same time, some wondered whether completing the profiles and assembling the portfolios would have been as meaningful without the narratives.

Joe Quattrini, one of the teachers in the study, said the writing of the narratives "takes an unbelievable amount of time to do. . . . Yet, without having to actually write the paragraph, it's almost too easy. Making circles [on the profile] makes for little cognitive dissonance, but writing the paragraph makes every number a judgment call."

Mary Sawyer, a researcher who reviewed the data from the study, agreed with Joe on the importance of the narratives. She found narratives "critical for interpreting the student's profile," valuable for revealing the influence of teacher-student relationships on performance, and useful to teachers' reflections on their own instruction. She was impressed in one teacher's narratives by comments on the need to "provide more support and encouragement to those students who choose to read very difficult novels, and . . . [to] keep [the teacher's] eyes open for literature that will appeal to students . . . who are interested in business." Mary concluded that the narratives have potential as a source of information not only for assessing student performance but also for improving instruction and supporting professional development.

The narratives at their best reveal not only the distinctive characteristics of the students' habitual performance but also the analytic process of the teacher in assessing the performance. Tricia

Hansbury-Zuendt's narratives on Sam's reading performance show her struggle to match Sam's performance to the performance indicators on the outcomes chart.

Reading for Personal Response   Level 2

When I read over Sam's writings describing his responses, his poor sentence structure and command of conventions leads me to think his work might be at a level 1, but those are not the behavior/products I'm evaluating here. . . . Sam reads very much for his own personal response. Often he sees a piece of literature in a way quite different from the rest of the class, or picks up on a detail that others discard. To him, that detail is significant and helps him make his own sense of the text. He reads better, responds more fully, when he can find something of his own life in a text, e.g., hunting in "A Sunrise on the Veld." Sometimes, unfortunately, I think he imposes his life experiences and their significance on the text a bit heavily, but he is intent on making his own sense of a text, in trying to bring it into his life. But because of his limited experiences he has difficulty reading a "wide range of complex texts" and so his main strength as a reader is also his weakness and limitation.

Reading for Information and Understanding   Level 1

I gave Sam a "complex and sophisticated" article by Joseph Campbell and he made sense of it using a guided questioning format (worksheet). Now, what do I call this, on our scale? *With direction.* Sam can read somewhat sophisticated material and make *some* connections between it, his own thinking, and other pieces he's read. (Does a blend of 1, 2, and 3 average out to a 2?) Actually I think he's performing at a level 1. He has difficulty telling me, *in his own words,* what Campbell's article is saying, although he can work methodically through the article. The phrase "in his own words" is significant; it implies (or would, if he could do it) a real understanding, however superficial. However, with discussion and guidance, his ability to make connections with other ideas allows him to gain an understanding of *these* ideas (Campbell's). I think his independent use of strategies (or lack of it) is what solidifies his level 1 rating.

Reading for Critical Analysis and Evaluation   Level 1

Sam can take a critical model, say, "The Fall from Innocence," and use the language of the model to explain a short story. He says of Ben, the young boy in Updike's "You'll Never Know, Dear . . . ," "Ben leaves home and goes to the carnival. . . ." and later in [Sam's] essay he writes that he believes Ben learns as a result of his new experience of the carnival (underlined words are from the model I gave the class). But his understanding of the events in the story seems incomplete. He believes the man at the gambling table is teaching Ben not to gamble, by being nice and giving him his money back, but misses the fact that the man doesn't give him all his money back. A problem here in reading for information and understanding, I guess, but it's directly related to his evaluation of the events. On the other hand, Sam goes on (unasked) and compares Ben to other heroes such as Perseus and Oedipus and what they learned. He says, "Other stories, like Perseus, Theseus, and Oedipus, were like an adventure, where this one was like a learning. What I mean is that in the other two stories, it was child to man, how he got there and how he was made. But in this story he stayed a kid and learned how to spend money." Now, this is not brilliant stuff, but he is trying to make some connections.

Tricia's narratives are lengthy compared to most of the others and tend to describe a specific example of the student's typical performance. On the other hand, Joe Quattrini wrote brief narratives that summarize the strengths of the student's habitual performance in each outcome. His narratives of Joan's performance in personal response and expression show the indicators Joe found most significant in assessing those outcomes.

Listening/Speaking for Personal Response and Expression
Level 3

As a listener, she is particularly sensitive to feelings and attitudes. As a speaker (most clearly evidenced in oral interpretations), she is effective in conveying nuances based on word choice and tone. Class presentations of poetic works and of her original writings show a clear "reading" of the text.

Reading for Personal Response   Level 3

Her response is sometimes so powerful that it overshadows the text, or, at least, the remaining text. Joan develops a very personal reading, but the reading sometimes becomes "solid" quickly, and then resists resynthesizing or development of other views.

Writing for Personal Expression   Level 3

Joan's expressive writing is strong on detail: "Set back on the quiet street, and the perfectly cut lawn led up to a small arched doorway." She is able to use descriptive and figurative language to set a mood for the reader. Her writing is conventional, but she writes effectively in a variety of expressive forms.

Joe's narratives capture a great deal of information in a very few words. Not only does he give a very specific picture of the student, but he clearly distinguishes the factors he focuses on for each outcome.

Some teachers didn't write separate narratives for each of the eleven outcomes but grouped the outcomes for reading, writing, and listening/speaking into three narratives. Ruth Townsend describes Maura's performance in listening/speaking in one narrative but includes references to different functions.

Listening/Speaking   Levels 1, 2, 1, 2

Speaking in front of a group is very difficult for Maura. She can speak on a limited range of topics but does her best on sharing personal experiences. Not surprisingly, her best performance in "Oral Communication," a ten-week senior elective, was her telling about the positive influence of her parents on her life. Maura's self-evaluation from her journal reflects her feelings about speaking in front of others. She is always very nervous, but she was less so with this presentation. Her other presentations were much more stilted, in part because she tried to rely on a written speech rather than on an outline for an extemporaneous presentation.

In small group settings, particularly where a specific task is to be tackled, Maura is an effective speaker, one who also assumes a leadership role, sometimes motivated by her desire to ensure successful completion of the group task. Again, her limited self-evaluation reflects her awareness of her comfort in small groups.

Like Ruth, Nancy Zuwiyya did not write separate narratives for each outcome but one for each domain: reading, writing, and listening/speaking. Nancy's narratives are also interesting because they contain considerable reflection on the process of assessment and on her instructional program along with the reflections on the performance of the students. In the midst of a lengthy narrative describing the reading performance of Frank, Nancy begins to describe a discrepancy between Frank's ability to read for personal response and his critical analysis of the same book, a discrepancy that leads her to reflection.

I don't believe his critical analysis was quite up to his actual comprehension of the book. And perhaps this is as it should be. When we encounter something very new, that doesn't fit the expected parameters of our knowledge, we need time to readjust, think, absorb, find new ways to redefine what we know. Maybe it will be next year when Frank will be ready to tackle this book in a critical and evaluative way.

I would suggest here that there may be a time lapse between the reading of a work and the ability to tackle it critically. We want students to try new and different things, but sometimes the territory is so new that all they can do is watch it go by. Perhaps, like true explorers, it will be in retrospect that they will analyze and evaluate the nature of their discoveries.

In other words, from my point of view, that fact that Frank struggled with something very challenging was of more significance than his ability to write about it with great sophistication.

The richness of the insights provided by these narratives led the reviewers to conclude that narratives should be included in any implementation of outcomes-based assessment. Like student self-assessments in recent portfolio projects (see especially Johnston [1992], Tierney et al. [1991]) writing narratives provides opportunity for the reflectiveness that is the most significant element in process classrooms. Admittedly, the logistics of implementing an outcomes-based assessment system that includes teacher narratives for each outcome are formidable and will require a commitment on the part of the school. As schools restructure to provide the best education for all students, they will need to develop schedules that give teachers more time to themselves and fewer students than most have now. In the meantime it seems important to use narratives to the full extent possible given teachers' present responsibilities, perhaps by sharing responsibility for the writing among more members of the faculty, spreading the writing over the course of a semester, or combining reflections on more than one outcome in a narrative as some teachers in the pilot study did. I hope we can avoid rejecting this valuable component of the process and returning to assessments that focus on what is easily measured and reported.

Teachers' Reflections

Every teacher in the project sent in at least a brief note commenting on the process, and some sent detailed reflections. The letters and notes gave a sense of the general feelings that the teachers had toward the project, and as seen above many narratives describing student performance also contained reflections on the process. All the teachers who completed the project reported that they found it satisfying and worthwhile. Even those teachers who called to say that they hadn't been able to complete the project commented on the positive experience of using the outcomes. Positive comments are encouraging, but more interesting to me are the problems and reservations the teachers expressed. These teachers are leaders in their field, and I am sure that any difficulties they experienced will be multiplied many times in the experience of the general population of teachers.

The Difficulties

Some teachers commented on the difficulty of internalizing criteria for each outcome. They mentioned spending a good deal of time just reading the charts of outcomes and performance indicators to develop their own sense of the distinctions being made and the behaviors indicated. One participant, Paul Feinstein, refers to the frustration he felt in dealing with the "conceptual nature" of the outcomes "because as a classroom teacher I am accustomed to dealing with specifics 95 percent of the time." Joe Quattrini seems to express the same frustration when he refers to the "vision" of the project as removed from his practical experience: "I'm not up there where panavision is even a possibility. The best I'm going to get—and the most important thing for me to get—is a *view*. Working in extreme closeup, writing eleven outcome reports for each of three people I've worked with for a few years."

Joe's comment on the practical orientation of classroom teachers led him, as he put it, "back to [Jonathan] Swift: 'Nothing is great or small, except by comparison.' " His realization that assessment relies on comparison was echoed in the comments of some of the others who remarked that in spite of trying to assess students with reference to the performance indicators rather than in comparison to other students, they found themselves thinking of the students in terms such as those used in college recommendations: "one of the best I have taught," "top 10 percent," "above average," "average". The same uneasiness was expressed by some as a desire for models or examples of performance at each of the levels.

A couple of teachers expressed a sense of dissonance between their own theories of language and those on which the outcomes were based. Tricia Hansbury-Zeundt questions the necessity of separate categories and wonders "in which ways the categories [are] all that different as one begins to apply them." Joe is troubled by what appears to be a "hierarchy" of outcomes with "critical analysis and evaluation" seeming to be "above the rest."

Almost every teacher commented on "the incredible amount of time" required to assess even three students this way and wondered how the process could be used for a full class without imposing an unacceptable burden on teachers.

The problems and difficulties pointed out by the teachers must be the central focus of continuing efforts to implement outcomes-based education and assessment. Ongoing conversation among teachers is the only way to come to agreement of what the outcomes need to represent and how they can be observed and reported in ways that are manageable and generally consistent in diverse classrooms.

The Advantages

In spite of their misgivings, the teachers expressed hope that a process of outcomes assessment could be implemented on a wider scale.

Every teacher offered to continue to work with other educators to help design a workable model of outcomes assessment. One teacher expressed a determination to use the outcomes for assessment during the next year with a whole class. Another commented that the project had helped her to "look at students' work and my own teaching a new way, and it's a way that seems to fit with my current philosophy." A teacher who described the process as "intimidating" found it nonetheless "healthful." Others called it "interesting" and "intellectually stimulating." Finally, teachers expressed the hope that outcomes assessment could lead to the kind of change in schools that teachers committed to process learning would like to see.

Questions of How and Who

Like all good investigations, this pilot study raised more questions than it answered. The biggest question was how schools can provide the necessary conditions for reflective assessment of habitual student performance. There is no simple answer to this question of how to provide the conditions for reflective assessment, but keeping the need in mind may help educators recognize opportunities for addressing it. Measures to facilitate outcomes assessment might include: planning schedules for an equitable distribution of students to be assessed (probably the graduating seniors at the high school and the corresponding classes of students at the middle and elementary schools), making use of shared teacher planning time to discuss student performance, making student "case studies" a regular feature of staff meetings, and having regular conferences with the parents of students in the group to be assessed. Any or all of these options might facilitate the process or outcomes assessment.

Related to the problem of providing conditions for reflective assessment is the need to provide for the participation of multiple observers. Teachers in the pilot study not only reported that they didn't have adequate time to do such reflective assessment of all their students, but some of them also felt that they needed to know how students performed as language users in other areas of their school and in their students' out-of-school lives. The English teachers were more than willing to have observations of other teachers and interested adults included in the assessment, but they acknowledged that providing for those other observations added to the complexity of the task.

Another big issue for some of the teachers and reviewers was the absence of an opportunity for student self-assessment in the pilot study. Joe Quattrini decided to involve his students in the process by having them help in the process of selecting portfolio pieces, writing narratives of their own performance, and reviewing what he had written about them. He says of this experience, "This is messy, but it feels like the right way to do things." Nancy Zuwiyya also felt that the omission of student self-evaluation was a weakness in the design of the assessment system. She says, "It seems to me that the three-part design . . . offers a great deal of potential, but it leaves out the student role in determining what it is he/she has actually accomplished and learned." But some others questioned student involvement in outcomes assessment. "Ultimately," Tricia Hansbury-Zuendt suggests, "performance has to stand up to the scrutiny of external judges."

Questions of What

What do the function categories indicate? One of the issues that emerged from the teacher comments was confusion about the function category that we had originally called personal response and expression. Several teachers and reviewers commented that personal response and expression is an element in all language use and the word *personal* did not reflect the kind of language performance described in the performance indicators for those outcomes. As a result of those comments, I have renamed that function category aesthetic response and expression, a term that the teachers and I agreed more clearly reflects the kind of language use intended. This change of names reflects the difficulty of defining discrete function categories. Actually, any language event is likely to be a mix of aesthetic, informational, critical, and social elements, but an awareness of the different qualities of language for each of those functions helps us as educators observe and improve performance.

What do the levels indicate? Some teachers reported difficulty thinking in terms of broad levels of performance and worried about differing expectations for those levels. Ruth Townsend expresses the frustration of trying to provide examples of student performance at different levels without any samples to guide her selection. In her reflections she writes, "Disturbing to me is my uncertainty as to what the definition for each category means. . . . I'd like to have several samples of [each of the levels]. Of course, I realize acquiring these samples is part of what this project is about and that my labeling . . . may contribute to clearer definitions of these assessment designations." Ruth's concern points up the difficulty of trying to assess student performance vis-a-vis standards of adult performance in areas where adult performance is never formally assessed. Publicly recognized standards of adult performance exist in areas of athletic and artistic performance, but in the area of language use, as in other areas of academic study, adults are not formally assessed and publicly recognized standards are not available. As Joe Quattrini puts it, "I'm driven to think of the whole population of communicators I've known. . . . What else can I use as the basis of judgment? I don't know how typical adults, whoever they are, write for critical analysis, or read for personal response, or speak and listen for information and understanding."

Uneasiness in ascribing student performance to previously undefined levels suggests that an important step in implementing outcomes-based assessment is to find some common understanding for levels of performance across all areas. Teachers may disagree, for example, about any individual's achievement of the level of exceptional proficiency of an outcome, but they should agree that it indicates habitual performance exceeding most mature performers in the field and reflects to a great degree the performance of the standard-setting professionals in the field.

What should teachers be assessing for listening and speaking? Almost every teacher referred to the relative dearth of evidence for evaluating listening/speaking performances of their students. Ruth Townsend referred to her assessment of listening/speaking as "subjective" and "impressionistic" for students who had not given formal oral presentations and raised the question about the implication of that for her curriculum, saying, "Perhaps this suggests that I need to build into my curriculum more opportunities for formal oral presentations, but I'm not sure about that." Other teachers relied completely on informal oral language experiences to observe listening/speaking performance. Galen Boehme describes students' performances in small-group discussions in the classroom and takes note of the ease with which the student adapts to different roles in the group. Of one student he says, "She can adapt well to any situation. . . . She will take the leadership—acting as a facilitator, a director, or a recorder— and then be able to synthesize the thinking of the group into some kind of coherent thought." Of another student he observes that she "works better in a group of two or three" but would "feel uncomfortable in presenting the ideas of the group to the entire class." The balance of formal and informal experiences in listening/speaking is a local decision, but the teachers' comments all suggest that more attention needs to be given to providing and observing opportunities in the school program for developing student "oracy."

What is the most useful way of focusing the narratives: individual outcomes, function, or domain? Teachers are used to thinking of language performance in terms of the domains of reading, writing, and listening/speaking. A review of the teachers' narratives reveals that, even in cases in which the teacher produced a separate narrative for each outcome, they sometimes referred to performance indicators that didn't match the particular outcome (such as commenting on the student's success with grammar exercises in the narrative for writing for social interaction). These examples of narrative/function mismatch suggest that focusing the narratives on the functions (aesthetic, informational, critical, and social) might help teachers to move out of traditional ways of thinking of language assessment and also provide greater insight into student meaning-making abilities. Mary Sawyer raises this question at one point in her review of the pilot study in reference to one teacher's narratives when she says, "The narrative may have been more coherent if they were organized around the functions." In her final reflections on the narratives she suggests giving teachers the option of how to organize their narratives. "Some teachers," she observed, "found it easier to write about the student using the [domains], Listening/Speaking, Reading, Writing. Perhaps others might have found it easier to organize their narratives into function categories without addressing the listening/speaking, reading, and writing skills separately."

What changes need to be made in the performance indicators to bring them in line with the teachers' knowledge of actual language performance? This was one of the central questions for us in launching the pilot study, but it remains an ongoing concern and will continue to be an issue as language changes and classroom practice and expectations change. Few teachers in the pilot study made specific suggestions for revising the performance indicators. Most of them accepted the performance indicators as written and looked for evidence of the given indicators in their students' performance. A few specific concerns about word choice were raised.

1. As mentioned above, the concern with the term *personal* was so general among reviewers and teachers that we substituted the term *aesthetic* in the labeling of the outcomes.

2. The term *objective*, used in the draft of the outcomes to distinguish considerations and criteria that are more public in nature, was objected to by several teachers and reviewers. As one reviewer pointed out, "No criteria are any more 'objective' than others since all derive from the values of a specific perspective."

3. Some questions were raised about the use of terms that refer to affective responses. What does it mean to "enjoy" or to "appre-

ciate"? What constitutes "the most satisfactory response"? All of these terms were used with reading for aesthetic response.

4. The particular focus of each function needs to be made more explicit in the narrative definition of the outcomes and in the performance indicators. This is especially true for the outcomes for social interaction. The performance indicators for writing and listening/speaking for social interaction need to be revised to focus on the interpersonal relationship indicative of these outcomes as distinct from the focus on the message in informational outcomes, on the critical perspective in critical outcomes, and on the personal response in aesthetic outcomes.

5. Reviewers who have seen the full eight-level continua have raised concerns about the terms used to make distinctions among elementary, intermediate, and mature levels. Some suggested that using the terms *children's literature* or *young adult literature* in the descriptions of levels of performance does not clearly indicate the nature of the material. Others thought that the term might be limiting. Interestingly, teachers who have reviewed the draft of outcomes recommend keeping those terms as indicative of a level of achievement but *not* of a particular age or grade. The same teachers remarked that the category of children's literature is not limiting but is as rich and diverse as literature intended for adult audiences. They were concerned that a desire to move children to a higher level of performance would result in children being moved out of that rich collection of children's literature too quickly.

What effect will this assessment have on curriculum? Another concern expressed by some teachers was fear that assessing student performance according to eleven separate outcomes could lead to a "disintegration" of the curriculum. Joe Quattrini raises this concern in his reflections: "What will keep teachers from creating new, disintegrated assignments so they will have the Information and Understanding Writing, the Social Interaction Writing, etc.? Just so as to make their judgment calls easier? And their teaching?" Tricia Hansbury-Zuendt's comments reflect the same concern as she refers to the tendency to look at each student product "as a separate example of a single outcome." As she says, "Old mindsets die hard." Nothing new will be accomplished if individual tasks (however complex) are assigned and evaluated to determine a student's performance on any outcome. Outcomes assessment requires observing in an individual's habitual performance evidence of proficiency in the desired outcomes, a significant difference educators should not lose sight of. It would be an unfortunate irony if the outcomes designed to facilitate assessment of student performance in an integrated program had the effect of disintegrating that program. In the next chapter I will discuss this central question of the relationship between outcomes and curriculum and instruction.

Summary

Participants

Twelve teachers from high schools in New York state and Kansas. Twenty-seven students had work included in the study.

Components

1. Language profile for each student with designations of the level of habitual performance for each outcome.
2. Portfolio for each student to support the teacher's judgment of the student's performance.
3. Narratives by the teacher describing the habitual performance of each student in each outcome.
4. Reflections on the process by the teacher.

Observations

- The outcomes assessment—with narratives, profiles, and portfolios for each student—provides a much fuller picture of the student as a language user than is available with traditional reporting measures.
- Specific criteria were necessary in cases in which the student performance seemed to be "between levels." In most cases, an internalized sense of the levels was sufficient to allow teachers to generate the profile.
- Broad levels of performance don't provide the capability for distinguishing degrees of achievement. To encourage and recognize student effort and accomplishment, some designation of degree of achievement might be included along with the level of performance.
- Outcomes assessment does not give the information about the academic experiences available in a transcript. Therefore, the outcomes report supplements rather than replaces the transcript.

- Narratives are valuable both to the teacher and to external reviewers, but they are very time consuming for teachers.
- When portfolios are used to provide evidence of habitual performance the samples of work are likely to be real pieces that contain evidence of a variety of different thinking and language abilities. They are not the artificial proxies for writing that might result if one were asked to include a particular product such as a persuasive essay.
- Portfolio collection, even of this limited type, is also a considerable addition to teacher workload.

Next Steps

- Involve more teachers in discussion to continue to revise the outcomes and performance standards so that they represent the consensus of informed professionals in the discipline.
- Continue discussion among teachers, administrators, and policymakers to develop the logistics of a manageable system of outcomes assessment.

The Pilot Study as a Beginning

The pilot study was the end of the beginning. The information provided by these experienced language arts teachers contributes to the ongoing revision of the outcomes and the process of outcomes-based assessments. Teachers, administrators, and policymakers at the local, state, and national levels continue to work together to design a plan for implementing outcomes-based programs and for agreeing on standards for student performance that will guarantee the highest level of achievement for all students.

Chapter Six

Instructional Programs

Achieving the twin goals of equity and excellence will require establishing outcomes for all students broad enough to be attained in a wide variety of ways. The language outcomes considered here are of such a nature. They refer in general terms to the language processes individuals habitually demonstrate without specifying the content of the reading, writing, or oral-language performances beyond those distinctions designated by the function categories: aesthetic, informational, critical, and social. Those outcomes can be achieved through local curricula that vary greatly in nature and prescriptiveness. Some schools will design programs that require all students to read the same list of "great books," write mandatory research papers and critical essays on prescribed topics, and participate in formal public-speaking courses. Other schools will help students to design individual programs that focus on the nature of the meaning making suggested by the outcomes. Either of those extremes, and anything in between, is conceivable for achieving the language outcomes, and most educators are willing to acknowledge that language ability can be developed equally well in a great variety of educational programs. However, when it comes to outcomes in other academic disciplines, tolerance for such flexibility is less common. There is a widespread perception that covering essential content in the other disciplines limits the possibilities for variations in the instructional programs. If only language learning allows for flexibility in designing programs, it is hard to see how schools can be restructured as radically as the reform movements are suggesting, or to see how prospects for intellectual achievement can be improved for students who are not successful in the existing system.

But what if process outcomes similar to language outcomes can be identified for all the types of learning educators value? Wouldn't such outcomes provide a grounding in the disciplines at least equal to what students achieve now without limiting the means of their attainment? I want to investigate the possibility of looking at the categories establisheded for language outcomes as fundamental aspects of meaning making that apply to learning of all types. Those categories might make a useful basis for expressing general graduation outcomes that can be achieved through the attainment of more specific program outcomes in a variety of combinations. In such a scheme the same general exit outcomes would be required of all students, but those outcomes could be met through program outcomes from a variety of disciplines. The outline that follows illustrates a model for connecting learning in a number of areas of the curriculum with broad statements of the desired learning outcomes. *Please remember it is an example only.* The statements of learning for the other disciplines are ones I found in a variety of publications and are used for purposes of illustration.

Graduation Outcomes

At graduation the student will demonstrate, at the acceptable adult level or higher, selected program outcomes that comprise the exit outcomes below.

Exit Outcome I:
Acquire and communicate information and understanding

Program Outcomes:

- Read, write, listen, and speak to gain and communicate information and understanding (English)
- Communicate mathematically (Math)
- Understand and discuss political, economic, and social issues in national and global society (Social Studies)
- Understand and discuss the natural world and its phenomena (Science)
- Gather information and make decisions as consumers of technological resources, products, services, and systems (Technology)
- Recognize and demonstrate understanding of a wide variety of art and music, including diverse styles and genres reflecting varied world cultures (Music, Art)

Exit Outcome II:
Respond and contribute to the aesthetic domain

Program Outcomes:

- Read, write, listen, and speak for aesthetic response to the artistic and cultural achievements of others and for personal artistic expression (English, Social Studies)

- Respond aesthetically to the natural world (Science)

- Use technology for aesthetic experience and expression (Technology)

- Participate in the appreciation and production of the fine arts (Fine Art)

- Participate in appreciation, production, and performance of the performing arts (Performing Arts)

- Respond to music emotionally, intellectually, and aesthetically and demonstrate creativity through music using skills in arranging, improvising, composing, and/or performing (Music)

Exit Outcome III:
Analyze and evaluate complex positions, issues, and trends

Program Outcomes:

- Read, write, listen, and speak to analyze, evaluate, and generate information and ideas according to personal and objective criteria (English)

- Reason mathematically (Math)

- Analyze and evaluate political, economic, and social issues in national and global society (Social Studies)

- Analyze and evaluate problems and issues related to the natural world (Science)

- Recognize, analyze, make informed value judgments, and take appropriate action regarding sociotechnological issues (Technology)

- Evaluate works of art using established criteria (Fine Art)

- Make aesthetic judgments based on critical listening and skills in music analysis, using music vocabulary (Music)

Exit Outcome IV:
Interact positively and productively with other people from diverse social groups

Program outcomes:

- Read, write, listen, and speak for positive social interaction (English)

- Perform music alone and with others and for self and others (Music)

- Work collaboratively to accomplish social purposes (General)

- Understand and live in accordance with the values and ethical standards of the community (General)

The outline above groups outcomes from a number of disciplines under four general categories. These particular outcomes statements appeared in publications in those disciplines; they are not inclusive of all the outcomes that might be described for those disciplines and do not even begin to address the outcomes of several other disciplines (health, physical education, second language). I present this outline to start a discussion of how general exit outcomes might be related to particular program outcomes, *not* to suggest the ultimate model.

The framework presented in the outline rests on the assumption that what is most valuable in education are the processes of learning and inquiry rather than specific content and products. If I had taken the opposite view—that the outcomes should be defined in terms of the products rather than the processes—a different framework than the one above would emerge. My framework is also dependent on the assumption that to a very great extent all learning is language learning, although some important areas of personal development are not accounted for in this scheme.

Frameworks for categorizing learning have been around since at least the time of Aristotle. Recent attempts to describe the scope of general education have resulted in a number of such frameworks. Some, like the Secretary's Commission on Achieving Necessary Skills (SCANS 1991) report, derive from what are thought to be the requirements of the workplace. Another general framework was proposed by the Carnegie Foundation (Boyer 1981) in 1981. Ernest Boyer describes in it six commonalities that could serve as a basis of general education. Other frameworks are similar to the one I am proposing in that they are related to language and literacy development. Probably the most comprehensive framework is still Michael

Halliday's list of the functions of language (1973). All of these viewpoints provide useful ways of looking at literacy and learning. The one I suggest has for me the value of being rather simple to understand and easy to relate to the curriculum.

My outcomes framework suggests that as students progress in various areas of the curriculum, they progress in the associated language outcomes. Language is not separable from the meaning making that occurs across the curriculum. Even in those areas of the curriculum in which another symbol system is learned and employed (math, music, dance, painting, drawing, and sculpture), verbal language is used in pursuit of that learning. This reality has important and somewhat contradictory implications for all educators and for English teachers in particular. First, it suggests that language learning is not the exclusive concern of the English class or the English program. Second, it suggests that English teachers should keep in mind the language demands of the entire school program in planning curriculum and instruction in the English language arts program. Finally, it also raises the question of whether language needs to be a distinct area of the curriculum.

A few years ago at a conference for reading and language arts teachers, Isaura Santiago-Santiago, the president of Hostos Community College, started her remarks to the assembled educators by announcing her belief that teachers should "stop teaching language in our schools." You can imagine the momentary consternation of the assembled language professionals. But Santiago's position reflects a view of language learning shared by many. Frank Smith (1988) states that language learning is "incidental"; that is, language is learned as it is used to perform an important function. Language is learned in the investigation of ideas and events of interest, in the attempt to explain our thoughts and feelings to others, in trying to enter into the fictive world constructed by another out of words, or in trying to sell an idea, a product, or a vision to others. Language is learned through negotiating meanings with other language users. Frank Smith's metaphor of the "literacy club" is a powerful one for language educators (1988), reminding teachers that we all learn most successfully those activities that we engage in freely, for our own purposes and with expectation of success. As students read, write, listen, and speak to investigate phenomena of nature and culture, they will develop their understanding of those phenomena *and* their proficiencies as readers, writers, listeners, and speakers, which is why Frank Smith describes language learning as incidental and why Santiago suggests that teachers stop "teaching" language. Rather than teaching language teachers must use language in the investigation of significant topics and concepts.

As educators, we do not have to agree that language should not be taught separately in order to recognize the wisdom of the position taken by Smith, Santiago, and others. Even if teachers believe in teaching English as a discipline with its components of literature, writing, and rhetoric, they may still agree that their focus should be on the meaning being made and the topics being investigated more than superficial elements of encoding and decoding. Instructors can also acknowledge that although the English class may allow opportunity to focus on language and its richness and possibilities in a way that is not found in other areas of the curriculum, a large part of student language development occurs in classes across the curriculum and in extracurricular activities. This belief could provide a basis for developing a curriculum balanced to provide wide-ranging experiences in each outcome through student participation in all areas of the school program. Instructional programs can be designed to provide multiple routes to the desired learning outcomes.

Experience in Aesthetic Language Use

Students use language to respond and contribute to the aesthetic domain in almost every area of the curriculum, but an especially important focus of the English curriculum is reading and responding to literature and writing literature in many forms. In English classes teachers provide aesthetic language experiences in reading, writing, listening, and speaking and can encourage attention to such experiences throughout the school program.

Writing in English Class

My own preference for focusing the curriculum is to begin with the writing experiences students will have. Certainly the same balance and breadth can be provided in a curriculum by focusing on the reading or oral-language experiences, and in some cases it will make much more sense to begin with either of those. For example, elective courses at the high school level defined by a literary period or genre (romantic literature or dramatic literature) will necessarily be centered around the works to be read, and those that are defined by the oral-language requirements (public speaking and debate) will focus on the listening and speaking with reading and writing in supportive roles. But in general, I find many benefits to making student writing the center of the curriculum.

The primary benefit to focusing on student writing is that writing gives students more authority over the meaning making in the classroom than necessarily occurs in the reading of literature by other authors or in oral discussion. The process of making decisions about substance and form engages student authors directly in the work of literary creation. When their works are presented to other students in the class, they are likely to defend the choices they made about what to write, to explain why they have selected particular literary devices to express their meaning, and to solicit responses of their audience about what works and what needs more attention. They come to know the craft of writing particular genres more easily and more thoroughly from attempting to write in those genres than from studying the works of other writers. The process is similar to young athletes learning to play a particular sport. Would-be baseball players learn more from picking up bats and gloves and playing ball than from watching and analyzing the play of even the most proficient players. My grandmother was an avid baseball fan and knew every player and the intricacies of the game, but she was not a baseball player and could not do any of things she so admired in the pros. People learn more about literary forms by writing in those forms than by reading them and talking about them.

The second benefit of beginning with writing, though, is that writing in particular genres promotes interest in the work of more accomplished writers of those genres. Many six- and seven-year-old children writing picture books in whole language classrooms have already selected favorite authors whose work they imitate, and they speak knowledgeably about the techniques of those authors. The same phenomenon occurs with junior and senior high school writers trying more sophisticated forms of writing. Budding playwrights turn to favorites among the professionals to learn the craft. Sonneteers, writers of ballads or epics, and science fiction writers all read the writing of other authors with a professional interest that far exceeds the attention of casual readers.

The critical attitude student writers take to published works is another benefit of starting with writing. Rather than reading published texts with the noncritical acceptance of the outsider, student writers are likely to be critical and discriminating. An experience with a senior class convinced me. Students recognize that the form and content of a finished work are the result of decisions made by an author, and they are likely to question those decisions and make judgments about their effectiveness. My students had been assigned to write stories based on a childhood recollection using a narrative perspective to convey the experiences of the young child most effectively. Shortly after that writing experience, the class read Joyce's *A Portrait of the Artist as a Young Man*. Their responses to the opening scene of the book were markedly different from those of other students with whom I had read it. While previous classes had experienced difficulty in getting into the text, this group immediately began to question who the narrator was in each section and why there seemed to be a shifting back and forth from a child's to an adult's perspective. Some of them were instantly struck with the possibilities of stream-of-consciousness writing (and they employed the technique in their future writing with great enthusiasm if not unqualified success), and some questioned the authenticity of the child's language. I am not suggesting that because these students were writers of similar stories they produced brilliant readings of A Portrait, but only that their experience of having tried to write similar stories made them willing to grapple with a difficult text and engaged them from the beginning in responses that were critical as well as interpretive. In my classes I found engagement in critical reading of literary works to be a natural result of having written in the same forms and an essential step in developing proficiency.

One way of planning a curriculum to provide increasingly challenging experiences in writing literary forms is to list forms students should experience and to divide these forms up as they might occur at different grade levels. One school district I know in New York state, Guilderland School District, has produced a complete chart of writing expectations for the district's K–12 program. In a simple-to-follow format, the chart maps out forms of writing students are expected to experience and indicates by capital letters the particular forms to be introduced each year. The chart for grades six through twelve appears in Figure 6-1. It provides a plan for instruction in a wide variety of writing forms, insuring not only that those forms will be included but also that there will be a progression from year to year. The chart indicates that students may be writing in some forms before they are formally introduced in the program, and they will continue writing in those forms in the years after they have been introduced. The chart does not limit the possibility for students to write in forms that appeal to them during any year, but it insures that they will have experience and guidance in writing all forms.

Reading in English Class

One note on the writing expectations chart from Guilderland School District indicates simply that "It is expected that students will have reading experience with each genre introduced." The district's statement says a lot. In a curriculum based on the writing experiences of the students, reading selections are made to correspond with the genres students are writing. For aesthetic reading, this approach means students read the literary genres they are writing (poems,

Middle School Writing Expectations
Grades 6-8

° CAPITALIZED items are to be introduced and are usually written two or more times in that grade

° It is expected that students will have reading experience with each genre introduced.

° To gain control of the descriptive mode, students will use words, phrases, sentences, and paragraphs that describe in most writing assignments.

	Expressive	Narrative	Expository	Persuasive
Grade 6	Personal response to literature Poem Paragraph of personal feelings and/or reactions to an experience or event Autobiographical sketch Friendly letter Journal entry	MYTH Feature article about a person Skit Folktale/Fable Short story Narrative of actual experience	NEWS ARTICLE How to article RESEARCH CONTENT REPORT Biographical sketch Book report Business letter	ADVERTISEMENT/COMMERCIAL Letter to persuade
Grade 7	Journal entry Friendly letter Poem Personal response to literature Paragraph of personal feelings and/or reactions	Short Story Feature article about a person or event Narrative of actual experience Skit Autobiographical sketch Myth	INFORMAL ESSAY News article How to article Research/content report Business letter BIOGRAPHICAL REPORT Character study bases upon work of literature	BOOK/PLAY/MOVIE REVIEW LETTER TO PERSUADE WRITTEN TO A REAL AUDIENCE Advertisement for a new product
Grade 8	Friendly letter Poem Personal response to literature Journal entry Paragraph of personal feelings and/or reactions	AUTOBIOGRAPHICAL SKETCH Short story Narrative of actual experience Feature article about a person or event	Informal essay News article PROCESS ESSAY Directions: How to do a task Research/content report Business letter CHARACTER STUDY BASED UPON WORK OF LITERATURE Biographical report Content report DEMONSTRATION SPEECH	Book, play, movie review Letter to persuade written to a real audience Advertisement for a new product

Figure 6-1
Writing Expectations: Guilderland School District

High School Writing Expectations
Grades 9-12

° CAPITALIZED items are to be introduced and are usually written two or more times in that grade

° It is expected that students will have reading experience with each genre introduced.

° To gain control of the descriptive mode, students will use words, phrases, sentences, and paragraphs that describe in most writing assignments.

	Expressive	Narrative	Expository	Persuasive
Grade 9	DESCRIPTION OF PERSON Friendly letter Personal response to literature through journal and essay.	Autobiographical sketch Narrative of actual experience	SUMMARY MULTIPLE SOURCE PAPER Essays News/feature articles	LITERARY ANALYSIS
Grade 10	Journal entry Familiar place essay Poems Personal response to literature	Personal narrative SCRIPT ADAPTATION Short story Myth Skit DIALOGUE	Multiple source paper Business letter of complaint Character study Summary ESSAYS: CAUSE AND EFFECT INDUCTIVE	Literary analysis Letter to editor Speech Review of event or performance PERSUASIVE ESSAY
Grade 11	Personal response to literature through journal and essay Poems	Personal narrative Script adaptation Short story Myth Skit Dialogue	ESSAYS: COMPARE/CONTRAST DEDUCTIVE Summary RESUME LETTER OF APPLICATION News/feature articles Multiple source paper	Literary analysis Speech Persuasive essay Review of event or performance
Grade 12	Personal response to literature through journal and essay Poems	Personal narrative Script adaptation Short story Myth Skit Dialogue	Essays: biographical, process, compare/contrast, foresight/hindsight, deductive, categorical, inductive Resume Letter of application News/feature articles Multiple source paper	Literary analysis SPEECH REVIEW OF EVENT OR PERFORMANCE Persuasive essay

Figure 6-1
(continued)

short stories, myths, and dialogues) as well as models of aesthetic responses (journals, interpretive essays, and literary analyses). The reading will help students understand and appreciate the conventions of each genre and learn the conventions of responding to those genres.

I do not mean to imply that reading literature is only done in the interest of learning to write literature; reading literature is more meaningful to people who have experience as writers of literature. The primary value of reading literature is the aesthetic experience itself, an experience of the meanings, associations, and feelings evoked by the words of the text. Stories, poems, myths, fables, and plays are read for their own sake, for the satisfaction of the lived-through experience. But every aesthetic reading of a text involves not only what Rosenblatt (1978) calls the "evocation" of the literary work but the interpretation and criticism of that evocation as well. When literature is read in the classroom, the focus is on students' responses, interpretations, and criticisms. Those responses, interpretations, and criticisms are likely to be richer and more well informed when students are writers.

Because reading literature is valuable in itself and not just as an adjunct to the writing program, the selection of texts for student readers deserves attention. As the note on the Guilderland writing expectations indicates, particular genres to be read in any year may be determined by the nature of the writing students are doing. But deciding on genre is only the first step in selecting classroom texts. There are many other considerations. What are the topics, situations, themes, and issues that have relevance for the particular students in your class? What cultural voices do you as a classroom teacher want to bring into the classroom discussion? What writers might be appealing to these students? What works will challenge students appropriately? What works, if any, do the community and parents expect these students to read? What personal favorites do you want to share with this group of students? What works do the students want to read?

I put the question of student preference last, but for many instructors today student preference is the starting point in selecting texts for classroom reading. Some degree of student choice in reading seems essential to help students become self-directed readers. Some teachers allow students to select books for outside reading while retaining to themselves the selection of texts for classroom reading and discussion. Others allow students to select from a limited number of texts and to read and discuss those texts with small groups of their classmates. In a few classes the choice is almost unlimited for required classroom reading as well as for outside reading. Balancing student choice with teacher guidance is a delicate procedure, but the variety of rich literature available in all genres and on all topics is so extensive that it should be possible to decide on works that meet the criteria of both teacher and students.

Selecting texts is an essential part of planning for aesthetic reading experiences. Although almost any text can be read from an aesthetic stance, poems, stories, novels, and plays invite and reward aesthetic responses in a way that other texts often do not. Finding works that deal with issues and ideas related to students' experiences and their evolving understanding of themselves and the world is an important teacher responsibility. Instructional responsibility also includes bringing in voices from many cultural groups, pairing texts selectively to provide for intertextual connections, and balancing traditional works with more contemporary ones. There are a number of resources available to help teachers select literature. One particularly useful one is Robert Probst's *Response and Analysis: Teaching Literature in Junior and Senior High School* (1988) which contains lists of works grouped according to issues as well as a discussion of response-based teaching of literature.

Listening and Speaking in English Class

The relationship between literature and writing in English class is well established and has received considerable attention over the years. The equally important relationships between oral language and writing and oral language and literature are less well established or investigated. Only recently has research focused on the importance of talk to the process of learning. The work of James Britton (1970), Douglas Barnes et al. (1990), and James Marshall (1988) has pointed out not only how crucial exploratory talk is but also how little substantive discussion among students actually occurs in the classroom study of literature.

A few years ago I did some research in the eleventh-grade class of Carol Reynolds, an outstanding English teacher whose classroom is response based and includes a great deal of student talk. As Carol and I watched the video tapes of the class meetings for the week I visited, we were both struck by the nature of the student talk we saw on the tapes. When students presented their personal responses to the literature they read, they were articulate and insightful and surprisingly original. But when they engaged with other class members in a discussion of literature, their language and thinking seemed limited and halting. What was intended to be group discussion on significant questions the students had raised about the text invariably ended up as rather stilted turn-taking in response to the questions. There was no elaboration of the comments by students who presented them, no probing of those comments by other students, no arguing out of divergent views. Certainly the presence of the camera and a visitor might have contributed to the restraint in the class, but the classroom talk we observed in those sessions led Carol and me to several hypotheses about classroom discussion:

- Students' personal responses are conveyed with an authority that indicates their confidence in themselves as readers and meaning makers, which argues for the value of starting with students' own responses in their own expressive language in all meaning making.

- The halting nature of students' language in group discussion suggests formal discussion is a form of discourse unfamiliar to students and requires a great deal of practice and modeling to acquire.

- The sense of discussion as shared meaning making is also not a practice students regularly experience. Formal instruction, guiding questions, and teacher modeling may all be required to help students learn how to think with other members of the community of learners.

- The startling difference between students' final written analyses of the literature and their classroom talk suggests that the benefits of that talk to the students' expanded understanding of the literature are much greater than is apparent from the conversation itself. The student papers the class produced were varied in form and content, but in general they were impressive in their insights into the work and the aspects of it considered in class. Whereas students didn't probe each other's thinking in classroom discussions, they did incorporate many elements of one another's questions and comments in their own final writing, often making connections among points raised or acknowledging the dissonance between readings from different perspectives.

Those observations convinced Carol and me that the classroom talk we had reviewed with such discouragement on the videotapes was valuable. Even though the discussion seemed halting and superficial, its influence on students' thinking about the literature was evident in their final writing. We concluded that rather than abandoning classroom discussion as an unsuccessful practice, we would be well advised to provide opportunities in class not only for students to discuss literature but also for them to learn about discussion through demonstrations of strategies and more consciously guided practice. Lee Odell, at a conference at the State University of New York at

Albany, proposed a model for guiding classroom discussion that gives students a few generic prompts to help them probe each other's thinking and their own. He suggests focusing students' attention on areas of consonance and dissonance among views presented. A simple outline that students can use during discussion appears in Figure 6-2.

Such a protocol need not be limiting. Students will quickly move away from the step-by-step process of asking each question and move to more spontaneous, elaborated discussion in which they probe the ideas raised by other members of the group. In literature study, sharing responses and ideas in group discussion may always sound tentative, which is the nature of initial readings of any complex literary work. Teachers become more comfortable with this type of discussion when they value provocative questions more than correct answers and original thinking more than consensus.

The students in Carol Reynold's class had developed a very effective practice for encouraging everyone to bring any questions they had into the discussion. After an initial period for raising significant questions that would lead to interpretation of the text, a time was set aside for raising "silly questions." During that time students could ask questions that might seem trivial or obvious to other readers. The inviolability of this practice became clear when one student raised a question that referred to the importance of a recurring image. Instantly, several students called out, "Not silly enough," and the

Figure 6-2
Protocol for Student Discussion

RECOGNIZING CONSONANCE

1. What areas of agreement do you find between your thinking and the ideas expressed?

2. What areas of agreement do you find between the ideas of this speaker (or writer) and other members of the discussion group?

3. What areas of agreement do you find between the ideas expressed here and other things you have heard or read?

ACKNOWLEDGING DISSONANCE

1. What areas of dissonance do you find between your thinking and the ideas expressed? Where do you disagree? What aspects had you not considered before?

2. What internal dissonance do you find in the thinking presented here?

3. What areas of dissonance do you find between the ideas of this presentation and the thinking of other members of the group? What disagreements? What differences in focus?

---

group refused to allow the question during that time. As an observer I could see the advantages of the silly question time for encouraging students to get a lot of thoughts onto the table without risking embarrassment. As one would expect, several (but certainly not all) of the silly questions turned out to be significant points for discussion. But it was not until I reviewed the students' work at the end of the project that the real value of the silly questions as a tool for shared meaning making became clear to me. The final papers convinced me that the silly questions help to maintain the tentative nature of the exploration by encouraging divergent thinking.

Aesthetic Language Use Across the Curriculum

Aesthetic response and expression is a primary focus in English class, but it is also central to other areas of the curriculum and should be present to some extent in all courses. In other "art" classes, students read, write, listen, and speak in response to artistic accomplishments in the fields of painting, sculpture, music, and dance much as they do in response to literature. The classroom practices described above are equally valuable opportunities for developing aesthetic response in these areas, and the connections are easily made. However, in subjects that belong to the sciences, both natural and social, it is also possible and desirable to provide opportunity for aesthetic response and expression.

The use of literature in social studies and science classes is becoming increasingly common as teachers investigate interdisciplinary connections. Students in American history classes commonly read works from the periods they are studying. However, the mere use of literary texts does not guarantee aesthetic experiences. Reading literary works in order to find information about the causes of the American Revolution, the death of Lincoln, or the conditions of life of enslaved Americans may provide valuable insights into those historical periods that can not be obtained from textbooks but, to the extent that the reader's attention is focused on the information to be garnered rather than on the lived-through experience with the text, such reading is an efferent and not aesthetic reading. Reading literary texts efferently in content-area classes is a valuable activity, but aesthetic reading may be even more valuable for immersing students in the cultures under investigation. Students who read widely and deeply in the romantic poets may become much more sensitive to the world view of the time of the French Revolution than students who study Dickens' *A Tale of Two Cities* to find details of the political situation. Likewise, students who enter into the fictive worlds of Skinner's *Walden Two* and Huxley's *Brave New World* may find personal connections with behaviorism that are more lasting and meaningful than the information to be gathered from scanning those works for principles of operant conditioning.

Writing for aesthetic expression is also valuable in content-area classes. In every class there are students whose preferred mode of making meaning is poetic rather than transactional. Howard Gardner's work on multiple intelligences has contributed to an understanding of the different symbol systems through which individuals express their intelligence (1983). Much professional writing in the natural sciences confirms the view that literary forms of writing are valuable for presenting world views of scientists. The writings of Stephen Jay Gould, Stephen Hawking, Richard Seltzer, William Carlos Williams, Loren Eisley, and Aldous Huxley come immediately to mind.

The same phenomenon is evident in social sciences. Hayden White in *Tropics of Discourse* (1985) makes the case that the forms of writing in history "have more in common with their counterparts in literature than they have with those in the sciences" (82). He argues that histories follow the same principle that Frye ascribes to poetry, pointing "in two directions simultaneously: *toward* the events described in the narrative and *toward* the story type or mythos which the historian has chosen to serve as the icon of the structure of the events" (88). Not all teachers of history and social studies will accept White's view of history writing, but most will recognize that students who write their own historical stories, poems, or plays are profitably engaged in structuring events and characters in plausible and meaningful ways.

Even in math classes students have occasion for aesthetic response. Rosenblatt (1978) cites a popular example in which "the mathematician turns from his efferent abstract manipulations of his symbols to focus his attention on, and to aesthetically savor, the 'elegance' of his solution" (25). Students who love mathematical puzzles and intricate geometric proofs and enjoy formulating and explaining them are involved in aesthetic language use.

Experiences in Informational Language Use

Writing for Information in English Class

A lot of writing students do in English class (and almost all of what they do in other classes) is informational writing. Expository compositions and reports that try to make sense of a topic for a particular audience (often the teacher) and investigative writing in journals and learning logs are extremely important to developing the ability to formulate and articulate meanings. Traditional classroom practice has tended to overlook the central importance of writing, treating it instead as an adjunct to the instructional program. Compositions and essays are occasionally assigned to test understanding of material or, more commonly, to test mastery of writing conventions. Teachers protest that there is not enough time for writing because there is "so much to cover." Writing that's not meant to be handed in or corrected is hardly even thought of.

The process view of writing has made a dramatic change in recent years in the amount of writing students do in English classes, but even in there teachers do not always see writing as an integral part of the meaning-making process, and the essential focus of informational language use—the focus on the message—is often ignored. Unfortunately, in some process classrooms the tendency may be to focus on the writing process and ignore the significance of the content, just as in traditional English classes the tendency was to focus on content and ignore the value of writing. Students need both a composing process and significant content to grapple with in order to become effective meaning makers and language users. A curriculum that relies on students' writing regularly to investigate and communicate information is essential to that development.

Writing to investigate thinking, commonly called "writing to learn," is often neglected in planning classroom experiences. There seems to be an attitude shared by many teachers as well as students that writing is a painful and demanding experience that should be kept to a minimum. This attitude is most common in teachers who do not write much themselves. Combined with this attitude is the frequently expressed belief that students will not see any value in writing that is not graded and "counted" in their average. Changing this belief requires establishing a climate in the classroom in which writing is regularly used by teacher and students to record and explore thoughts and ideas before those thoughts and ideas go public. Journals and learning logs, brainstormed lists, written comments in response to classroom experiences and presentations, brief summaries or reflections at the end of the class, and questions and comments on work done for homework all help students form their own thoughts and contribute to the shared investigations of the class. *A Community of Writers* by Steven Zemelman and Harvey Daniels (1988) contains excellent suggestions for writing-to-learn activities that make writing a natural part of classroom activity. Students are engaged in ongoing writing activities that have real purpose and value for the students but do not add to the teacher's "correcting" burden.

The kind of investigative thinking students do in writing to learn is essential to writing of all types. One of the most obvious reasons for the unsatisfactory quality of much writing (not only students' writing) is failure to recognize that writing is most importantly "a process of discovery and interpretation" (Berthoff 1981, 20). Some opportunity for exploring one's own thinking on a topic is necessary before presenting that thinking to an audience. When writing "goes public," it is always "oriented toward the response of the other" (Bakhtin 1986, 75), and the relationships among the writer, the audience, and the subject help to give it form. Good writing, then, relies on the investigative practices that students develop in the writing-to-learn activities and on experience in fitting their language, style, form, and message to particular audiences. The ability to write for a variety of purposes and audiences depends also on control over a wide range of language conventions and forms. Experience in writing regularly to investigate a wide variety of ideas, events, and feelings helps students gain that control while they are acquiring an ease of expression and a personal style and voice.

In my classroom I tried to provide opportunities for students to write on the same topics or themes for different audiences and purposes in order to increase their own understanding of the topic and to develop flexibility in using different language forms. But it is essential that those purposes and audiences be realistic. I once had a student who was an extremely reluctant writer but an accomplished auto mechanic. To encourage his development as a writer, I sometimes suggested that he write explanations of maintenance procedures for those of us in the class who knew less than he about cars. The writing that he did for that audience was really not bad. In spite of poor spelling and punctuation, he presented rather clear explanations of the parts of a car and steps for keeping them in shape or doing minor repairs, and he did it in language easily understood by a layperson. However, when I suggested he write on the same topic for an imagined audience of other auto mechanics, the writing seemed to fall apart. The suggestions were poorly developed and had none of the practical examples—"If your battery seems [dead] and it is not bitter cold out, you probably left your lights on"—that he included in pieces for the nonmechanics in the class. At that time I credited the weak quality of the writing for the more knowledgeable audience to his lack of language competence, but I think there is another explanation. The task I set for him in writing an explanation of car repairs for nonmechanics made sense to him. He could see that he knew something that we didn't, and he found satisfaction in explaining those mysteries to us in language we could understand. In today's terminology I might say that I had given him an "authentic" task. On the other hand, the request to write the same type of explanation for other mechanics made no sense to him. Why would a self-taught amateur, albeit a good one, write a manual for mechanics more experienced than he? Maybe the bare-bones directions and undeveloped statements of those weaker pieces did not result from either an unwillingness to approach the topic from that perspective or a lack of language but a sense that he had nothing valuable to contribute to that audience on that topic.

I think my experience with that one young writer contains a significant point for evaluating academic writing assignments in general. Far too often school writing assignments require the students simply to "write about" a topic. When the only audience is the teacher—who already knows a great deal about the topic—the task is likely to seem artificial to the student. Here are some possibilities for providing opportunities for "real" informational writing in English class.

1. Find real audiences for the writing. Classmates, younger students in the school, and community members who may not know about a topic can all be audiences for writing produced in the class.

2. Help the writer find a personal slant on the topic. Parroting back information held in common has little value to anyone, but adding to the knowledge in the class by contributing information not available to everyone or providing new perspectives on a topic is worth devoting time and energy to.

3. Encourage exploratory writing that investigates possibilities rather than offering conclusions. Often school writing is aimed at presenting the correct view of information, which for the student comes to mean remembering what a text or another authority said on the subject and repeating it correctly. Very different writing might result from asking students sometimes to write to explore many possible interpretations of the same information without needing to decide on one as superior.

4. Encourage writing on the same topic from different perspectives. The growing awareness of the cultural diversity in our society has made teachers conscious of the significance of perspective. Perspective is, of course, the essential element in the process of forming critical judgments, but perspective is also responsible for determining what information individuals focus on and what significance they assign to particular information.

5. Invite students to use classroom writing as an opportunity to enter the conversations going on among writers in their textbooks

and other professional materials, their teacher, and other students of the topic. To start this process students might be asked to identify areas of agreement and disagreement between their own thinking and the thinking of others in the conversation (as suggested in the model for small-group discussion). Starting from the question, How does this information fit in with what I previously thought about this topic? can help students make their own meaning when writing on topics that are part of classroom study.

The last suggestion is one that I think is especially important. In attempting to make writing assignments "real," teachers sometimes think they must connect the assignment with practical matters outside of school. I would argue that academic investigation *is* real and has considerable value for most members of our society. Inviting students into ongoing discussions on questions of importance within the academic disciplines is a most effective way of developing their understanding of those questions. It is different from telling students what we as teachers think or what others think about those issues and requiring them to give that thinking back to us in their writing. Berthoff (1978, 1981), Bartholomae and Petrosky (1986), Elbow (1986, 1991), Mayher (1990), and Slevin (1988) offer specific suggestions for providing opportunities to engage students in significant writing within all the disciplines they study. In English class much of that writing may be in response to literary texts but, because of the particular interests of the students and teacher, it may also be on topics that cross over into other areas of the curriculum.

The variety of forms for informational writing is extensive. Using a plan such as the Guilderland High School model for formal instruction in particular forms of writing each year gives students opportunities to discover the significant features of different forms and structural patterns. Experience with a variety of traditional forms helps students to discover effective ways of expressing relationships among aspects of a topic—relationships of cause and effect, similarity and difference, temporal sequence, and generalizations and specific instances. In English classes the diversity of topics and consequently the diversity of forms of writing is limited only by the imaginations of the community of writers in the class.

Reading for Information in English Class

The reading/writing connection is an essential feature of a process classroom, and in the area of informational language that reading and writing connection is especially strong. Reading for information in

English class includes reading other students' papers, reading works of professional writers that students encounter in their research, and—I hope—reading writing by their teacher. The first two sources of readings may seem obvious by now for a classroom centered on students as meaning makers, but I have not yet paid much attention here to the importance of the teacher's full participation in the activities of this community of learners. It is commonplace to point out that teachers in any field should be active participants in that field: piano teachers should play piano, tennis teachers should play tennis, science teachers should be involved in scientific investigation, computer teachers should use computers, and literature teachers should read and/or produce literature. Thus, writing teachers should write and should share their writing with student writers in their classes.

Sharing each other's writing in writing groups in the English class is a common practice for providing audience feedback during the writing process. Many texts describe practical strategies for developing effective student writing groups (see especially *In the Middle* [Atwell 1987] and *A Community of Writers* [Zemelman and Daniels 1988]). But another effective use of student writing is recommended by Bartholomae and Petrosky (1986) who use autobiographies of students as case studies in their writing course, in which one focus is "Growth and Change in Adolescence" (36). Other programs use collections of student essays on themes of the class or collections of student poetry and fiction as texts for classroom study. "Use of writing to help with the ongoing inquiry in the class," Zemelman and Daniels point out, "counts as an important kind of publishing" for student writers and, I would add, an opportunity for expanding the knowledge and understanding of student readers.

Sometimes teachers hesitate to use student writing as texts for classroom inquiry into significant topics for fear that student texts will be limited or even inaccurate in their consideration of the topic, a fear that points out the importance of placing student writing within a larger context of the work of professional scholars and writers. Including reading of professional writing on a topic helps to insure access to fuller information and provides opportunities for students to learn how to use the ideas of others in their own writing. Bartholomae and Petrosky (1986) describe the value of these opportunities.

> We are . . . preparing our students to carry out that complex negotiation where a reader or writer uses the work of others, neither his equals' nor his colleagues', to enable work that he can present as his own. There is an immediate, practical lesson here as well, for it is at

this point that we can begin to help students sort out the mysteries of quotation, paraphrase, citation, and plagiarism. At this point the lines are in a sense cleaner, since students are prepared to see how someone else's ideas fit into a project they themselves have begun. . . . They are in a position to see how the words of another can function in their own arguments: providing key terms; providing examples of statements that help authorize what they, too, would say; providing examples of statements that can be shown to be limited or inadequate. (Bartholomae and Petrosky 1986, 37–38)

Reading the texts of professionals and learning to use material from those texts effectively and responsibly in their own writing is indispensable to developing students' proficiency in the types of writing commonly used in academic study. But again I do not want to suggest the reading is done solely in the service of the student writing. Students read works by many professionals in order to advance their own understanding of a topic. If educators want students to grapple with the full complexity of issues and topics of particular interest to them, they have to give them opportunities to read primary texts on those topics. Psychology students who become interested in Freudian theory should read Freud as well as the writing of psychologists who have written about Freud. Students should not be confined in their academic investigation to the textbook and the encyclopedia. One reason for the shallowness of student understanding of complex issues may be a lack of direct access to the original thinkers. Often the only material available to students on a topic is a watered-down textbook explanation or a bare-bones summary in a general reference book. Neither source represents exciting writing or provocative thinking! Providing opportunities for reading scholarly works requires considerable skill on the teacher's part in helping the student to choose manageable topics and materials. If, like me, you are committed to negotiating the curriculum with your students as recommended by Garth Boomer (1982), then you know the importance of providing information that guides their choices and of renegotiating when a project proves to be too difficult. In such a climate of negotiation, students can tackle challenging topics and materials without fear of being penalized for taking a risk. They gain authority over complex and demanding texts as they expand their knowledge and understanding of the topic.

Listening and Speaking for Information in the English Class

In traditional English classes and in teacher-centered classes in every content area, most of students' time is spent listening to the teacher talk, and that talk is almost always intended to transmit information. In student-centered classes students are actively engaged in meaning making. In those classrooms I usually expect to hear less teacher talk and, maybe, somewhat less talk in general as more class time is spent on writing and reading. But just the same, in the student-centered classroom there will be a great deal of talk, most of it by students themselves either as individuals presenting ideas to the whole class or in pairs or small groups discussing topics and issues under investigation. The talk among students and teacher about topics of interest constitutes a class as a community of learners. Rather than sitting silently next to each other listening to the same teacher voice, students are involved in ongoing conversations. Many of those conversations might follow the suggestions for classroom discussion in Figure 6-2 on page 123 in which students exchange ideas on a topic, raise questions for each other, and identify areas of consonance and dissonance. In other instances students listen while a classmate presents findings from an investigation of a topic and then ask questions of the presenter to expand their understanding. Some talk will be responses to a student's reading of a draft of a paper. Informal conversations make up the majority of the listening and speaking in the classroom, but there are occasions of more formal oral presentations by students and teacher.

The formal listening and speaking opportunities for students in the classroom might include panel discussions, oral reports, readings of completed papers, readings from professional writers, and formal speeches. Such experiences provide student speakers with alternative modes of presenting their thinking to the class and with practice in using conventions of formal oral language. They provide student listeners with practice in listening to acquire and interpret information presented orally, a crucial skill for participating in the public life of our increasingly oral society. The option of oral presentation for some of the students' academic reports encourages the development of oracy and accommodates students for whom speaking is a favored mode of expression.

Even in student-centered classrooms there is a place for teacher talk. For one thing the teacher's voice is an important component in the ongoing classroom conversation. When it is not the only voice or the dominant voice, it may actually become a more valued voice. We as teachers are discovering what many parents have long known: when we speak seldom and briefly we command more attention than when we talk constantly. Nancie Atwell's suggestion (1987) of the "minilessons" of five minutes or so has proven itself to teachers who have tried it. I once visited the classroom of an eighth-grade teacher who had a double period of reading/writing workshop. After a brief break at the midpoint of the class, he called the students back to work by directing their attention to the board where he had written three sentences. "Many of you are putting dialogue into your writing now since Aaron started writing his story completely in dialogue. There is something you need to know when you are writing dialogue." He then proceeded to explain to them the rule for punctuating nouns in direct address when they come at the beginning, middle, and end of the sentence. After going over each of the three examples on the board, he concluded by saying, "I'll be coming to talk with you about your writing. If you have any dialogue that includes the name of the person being spoken to, show it to me and I will check to see if you have used this rule right." The explanation took less than five minutes, the students all paid attention in a way that reminded me of athletes listening to a coach during a game, and they all started looking through their writing for examples of the rule as soon as the minilesson ended. As someone who spent whole periods "teaching" that rule and others like it early in my career, I was struck by the efficiency and the effectiveness of this succinct lesson.

Teachers' voices are also valued because the teacher has knowledge and experience useful to students in their investigations. When the teacher's knowledge is seen as a resource, students can decide how much input to request from the teacher, which questions they need help with, and what kind of feedback from the teacher will help the student's self-assessment.

Informational Language Across the Curriculum

Everything that is true about informational language in English class applies to informational language in all other areas of the curriculum. In fact, the English teacher is well advised to have the role of language in the other disciplines as a model for English class. In the other subject areas the focus is likely to be on the message—the investigation of the topic or idea—with the quality of the language determined by how successfully it contributes to that investigation and by how well it adheres to the conventions of that discourse community. Using the standard form for phrasing a geometric proof in math class or for proposing a formal hypothesis in science class is an indication of the student's grasp of the processes for making meaning in that discipline.

The essential question for teachers in every class to keep in mind is, Who is doing the thinking? Are students writing and speaking to explore their own thinking on a topic and to explain that thinking to an audience, or are they writing and speaking to repeat the thinking of the teacher or the textbook? James Slevin (1988) suggests that learning any discipline means entering into the ongoing conversation that constitutes that discipline through "writing within disciplines." He mentions several critical questions students face in trying to enter the conversation.

> How do you learn to read so that you can enter this history, join this dialogue? How do you learn to write so that you can shape this dialogue, effecting assent, disagreement, further questioning, and so on? In other words, how do you learn to write so that your writing elicits other writing? Learning to respond critically and to summon such response from others is what it *means* to learn a discipline, for this is how a student, through such reading and writing, joins the historical dialogue. (Slevin 1988, 12)

Slevin's model of schooling fits in well with the critical, participatory learning proposed by the Brazilian educator Paulo Freire. Freire's own explanation (1987) of the relationship between learning to learn and learning particular subjects is helpful to understanding the concept of "critical literacy."

> From the progressive teacher's perspective, teaching students how to learn can never be reduced to some operation where the goal is merely how to learn. Teaching someone how to learn is only valid in a progressive class when the learners learn how to learn as they learn the inner meaning (the raison d'être) of an object or subject of study. It is by teaching biology or economics that the teacher teaches students how to learn.
>
> For progressive teachers, pedagogy implies, then, that the learners penetrate or enter into the discourse of the teacher, appropriating for themselves the deepest significance of the subject being taught. The indisputable responsibility of the teacher to teach is thus shared by the learners though their own act of intimately knowing what is taught. (Freire 1987, 213)

The "act of intimately knowing what is taught" Freire refers to involves students in speaking and writing their own meanings. In content-area classes, as in English class, students begin by talking with other people whom they trust about topics of interest to the class —looking for significant ideas and events, probing each other's understandings, raising questions, offering bits of information from their prior knowledge, responding to the thinking of others—and through all of these conversational activities the students increase their own understanding of the topic under investigation and contribute to the increased understanding of others in the conversation. Closely connected to this classroom talk is explanatory writing. Britton explains the relationship between classroom talk and writing in this way:

> Talk has a heuristic role to play, and expressive talk (being relaxed talk, relatively free from fear of making errors) is likely to be more strongly heuristic than, for example, the more formal exchange of teacher question and student answer with a whole class as audience. But (a) writing, as premeditated utterance, may have the effect of sharpening the process of seeking relevance, as well as harvesting for the writer connections first explored in speech, his own and other people's. And (b) writing puts the onus for effort on each member of the class. Hence the hypotheses that expressive writing has an important role to play in the initial stage of grappling with new concepts. (Britton 1982, 125–6)

The formal, public writing students do in content-area classes relies on the informal talking and writing described above. Teachers expect that as students think together about a topic and take their own notes to record similarities and differences in the ideas expressed, patterns will emerge in students' thinking and they will be ready to pull their thinking together and compose it in a suitable form. There are times when the teacher will suggest a form for students' formal writing on a topic but, as students become more assured writers, an important step in the writing process is finding the form that allows them to express their thinking most effectively for the intended audience. When the audience is assumed to be other participants in the professional conversation of that discipline, students will want to use the forms valued within that discipline. Students working on drafts of this kind of writing will try out the drafts on other students and the teacher. Feedback from these other students and comparisons of their writing with other writings being read in the class, both professional writing and student writing, will help students determine what constitutes "good writing" in the context of this particular class.

Peter Elbow (1991) also suggests that teachers could give students some informal "speak alouds" of their reactions as they read sample student papers, commenting on the effect that certain passages might have on different audiences. He gives some examples of the type of comment that might be made: "I am bothered here—I'll bet most teachers would be—but perhaps general readers wouldn't mind," or "I liked this passage, but I suspect a lot of teachers would take it as an inappropriately personal digression—or as too informal or slangy." The purpose, Elbow argues, is not to "teach the students the particular conventions they will need for particular disciplines" because he says that can't be done, but to teach them the principle of "discourse variation" so that they will be sensitive to the different standards and conventions they will find as they go from teacher to teacher and class to class.

Experiences in Critical Language Use

Writing in English Class

Critical reviews and critical analyses are common types of writing in English class. In the study of literature students produce critiques of literary pieces, and in the study of writing they often analyze an issue and write a piece taking a position on the issue. These common types of classroom writing are certainly examples of critical thinking and writing (or could be), but I think it is helpful to think of critical writing in the broader sense that Ann Berthoff alludes to when she claims that "teaching writing is a matter chiefly of teaching critical thinking" (1981, 113). Berthoff defines critical thinking as "the capacity to see relationships methodically" (114). A focus on relationships suggests that every developing idea, concept, opinion, and interpretation comes from a particular perspective and takes its particular shape from the value structure of that perspective. Her ideas sound abstract and vague, but it may be helpful to recall the questions considered previously for guiding classroom discussion. Such questions as, How does this fit in with what I already know? or How do the ideas of this speaker agree or disagree with my own? are a first step toward recognizing the value systems that underlie opinions and perceptions.

When students encounter differences of opinion in classroom conversation or in their reading, they try to explain those differences by what they know of the person expressing the opinion. They recognize that all speakers and writers are situated in particular contexts with significant personal, professional, and cultural aspects. While they may not be able to account for the particular perspective of every writer or speaker they encounter, they often are able to do so with the writers they know best: their own peers and classmates. They can more easily account for differences between their own perspectives and those of their classmates because they know a lot about those classmates and the groups with which they identify. For example, students writing about the issue of gun control may be surprised to find that a classmate who shares many of their views differs from them in his resistance to gun control. But they may be able to account for that difference in perspective when they recall that the dissenting student is a marksman and a hunter.

Beginning with a recognition of differences in perspective among members of a class or writing group helps students develop an awareness of the relationships between a writer's views and the value system of the cultural group in which the writer is positioned. Extending that critical awareness to views students encounter in the writing and speaking of other thinkers in the discipline requires that the student try to discover the cultural codes in which those thinkers are situated. They can ask about a writer or speaker, Whose interests does he have in mind? or What group is she speaking for? And even though they cannot carry on a real conversation with those thinkers, they can use their own writing and thinking to try to discover those relationships.

The most important writing that students engage in to develop their critical thinking ability is exploratory writing that continues the conversation with other thinkers in the discipline. The use of a dialogue journal, also called a double-entry notebook, can provide a vehicle for that conversation. The journal is useful for note-taking during classroom lectures or discussions and for responding to assigned reading. It provides space on the right-hand side of the page to write down what the "other" says and on the left-hand side for students' own questions, counterarguments, translations, and connections. Through the use of the journal, students are led to identify and understand relationships and to recognize "how judgments and opinions, generalizations and interpretations, are related to context and perspective" (Berthoff 1981, 115), and most importantly they begin to discover what their own value system is, where it comes from, and how it affects their judgments.

In writing for critical analysis, students are made aware of the significance of language and word choice. They begin to recognize that words are not neutral conveyors of objective information, but that a specific choice of words identifies a writer as a member of a group with a particular perspective. That point was brought home to many educators during the preparations for the five-hundred-year anniversary of Columbus' voyage when we became aware of the significance of calling his landing a "discovery," the people he encountered "Indians," or the effect of the white explorers on the natives "civilizing."

One of the questions that student writers should continually ask themselves is how the meaning changes when they change the wording (Berthoff 1981). Political critics have made us aware that all language is ideological, that there is no neutral or objective language free of cultural values and assumptions. Feminist critics in particular point out cultural assumptions embedded in our language, arguing that "the language we speak and write has been an encoding of male privilege . . . inadequate to describe or express women's experience" (Ostriker 1985, 315). Students now belong to a generation that has been sensitized to the exclusivity of expressions like "mankind," "history," and "mastery," and they are likely to be more aware than their teachers were at their age of the effects of such word choice.

One classroom procedure that helps focus students' attention on the ideological content of their language is to have each member of the class bring a piece of writing to a writing group and ask the group to respond to each piece by saying what attitudes or values are suggested by the language of the piece. Students then revise their work and bring it back to the group for the same kind of response. The process may be repeated several times while students struggle to find the exact wording to convey attitudes and values they want in the piece. Students are always surprised to discover through such a process that words they thought were objective or neutral suggested a particular bias to some readers.

Another classroom procedure for focusing student attention on the ideological content of language is group writing. A small group of students is given the task of writing an opinion on a significant issue to be presented to the rest of the class. The process of deciding on wording among the group members provides considerable discussion of the import of particular words and phrases. When the piece is presented to the class, the class responds as the groups did to individual pieces on the attitudes and values revealed in the piece. The writing group may then try to revise to achieve the effect they want.

Reading in English Class

In discussing critical language it is clear that reading, writing, listening, and speaking cannot be separated. The activities described above for providing opportunities for students to use writing for critical thinking rely as much on reading and listening and speaking as on writing itself. Close analysis of writings of members of the class is an exercise in critical reading as well as in critical writing. In writing groups students have the opportunity to talk with the writer of a piece and point out meanings they are finding in the text and indicate where the language seems misleading, imprecise, inflammatory, or confusing. Active dialogue enables the reader/listener to ascertain the position of the writer/speaker more clearly through the give and take of the conversation and to indicate to the writer where the language fails to communicate that position.

As discussed above, the writer uses responses of members of the writing group to guide revision of the text until the language expresses the writer's meaning as fully as possible. During this process the other members of the group who are the readers of this particular text are also refining their own thinking on the issue by questioning the writer's position and discovering similarities and differences between the writer's perspective on the issue and their own.

Such a procedure is also valuable for students reading professional texts. The dialogue journal provides a mechanism for them to grapple with underlying assumptions and values of passages from assigned readings and to try to discover the "position" or context of the writer of that text as they did with their fellow students. Recognizing the values and attitudes underlying professional texts in the class is much more difficult for students than doing the same kind of analysis of texts written by their classmates. Unlike the writing of their peers, the professional text may well be all students have to go on; they not only cannot question the writer directly as they can with their classmates, but they also may not know anything about a writer, the writer's context, or any other of his or her writings. Nevertheless, the experience students have in probing each other's writing and thinking will help them discover meanings and values in other texts they read and will enable them to recognize tensions between their perspectives and other writers'.

It may sound too obvious to insist that the nature of the texts students read critically is of primary importance. The process of questioning the values and attitudes of an author and differentiating the author's perspective from one's own is only rewarding when reading a piece of "real" writing, a text intended for a real audience and a specific purpose. Readers cannot have a meaningful dialogue with a summary from a study guide or a passage from a textbook, where the language has been sterilized and simplified to the extent that no personal meaning is included. Readers can only have a dialogue with another thinker. An important role for teachers is to help our students find texts that will involve them in increasingly challenging and rewarding conversations.

I started this section by trying to expand the understanding of critical reading and writing beyond the literary critique, but I do not want to ignore that genre. I recognize that much of the criticism students do in English class is part of their aesthetic experience of texts. Because that literary experience is a valuable part of the curriculum for all students, I want to place special emphasis on students' experiences in literary criticism.

In the literary transaction, Rosenblatt (1978) suggests the critic will often ask, "How did the specific elements of the text lead me to create that particular experiential work? . . . Or what aspects of the text explain my sensing a voice, a style, that seems unique to that author?" (162). At the same time the critic might ask, What past experiences or cultural values cause me to focus on specific elements in this text? and, How does my reading of this text change when I purposely shift my perspective to the codes of another group with which I identify? We might ask, as Judith Fetterley recommends in *The Resisting Reader* (1978), what happens to my reading of Hawthorne's "The Birthmark" if I purposely revisit that text from a feminist perspective rather than reading it only from the perspective of a literature student who admires Hawthorne's style? In examining the relationships between the cultural codes of the text and the cultural codes of the readers, students will use and acquire the language of literary scholars. In some cases the language and concepts of literary study are a major focus of the course; in others, acquisition of the language of literary scholarship is incidental to classroom investigation of literary texts. In either case students who are involved in literary criticism in their classrooms acquire both the language and the "habits of mind" of professional critics.

Critical Language Across the Curriculum

In the study of literature and in every discipline students are acquiring the particular language of scholars as they are using that language to investigate relationships between aspects of texts that they read in class and concepts of major concern to professionals in the discipline. In studying the sciences, for example, students not only learn the names of phenomena they are investigating but they also learn some central concepts of the discipline (validity, falsifiability, hypothesis), and they use those concepts to make judgments about data and issues under investigation in class.

An important aspect of learning in content areas is recognition of different schools of thought within those disciplines. As in the case above in which students in English class looked at authentic texts from different perspectives and dialogued with those texts through their journals, students in content-area classes can discover relationships among the views of a variety of thinkers on questions of interest to the disciplines they are studying. Through critical reading in a variety of texts, students come to realize that certain questions are "issues" of significance to a field precisely because they are seen and explained differently by different thinkers, but such complexity of thought may elude students whose reading is limited to the textbook. Determining their own positions on those issues and distinguishing their positions from those of their classmates and teacher—and from the professional writers—is the essence of critical thinking and language.

Experiences in Social Language

Language for social interaction is the most likely language function to be ignored in the school curriculum. Teachers readily acknowledge the importance of providing experiences for their students to use language for aesthetic, informational, and critical purposes, but many question the need or value of focusing on student social language use. Teachers assume students have opportunities every day in their homes and neighborhoods to talk with other people in a variety of social situations and to learn the customs of carrying on conversations in those situations. Most students do have some such opportunities, but few have regular experience of social conversation with people of diverse backgrounds and cultural groups.

The school community brings students into social contact with a variety of people they may not encounter in their own homes and neighborhoods, and providing opportunities for them to talk together is an important contribution to their development. It is a tradition as old as coeducational schooling that many boys first learn to talk to girls (and vice versa) in school. It is an often-lamented reality of school bus riding that young children first learn the language and behavior of older children on those endless daily treks. It has been the earnest hope of many immigrant parents for generations that their children would acquire the educated speech of their teachers through daily classroom conversations. All this learning of social language does take place and is a valuable part of schooling, but educators cannot trust to chance that students will gain access to all the forms of language they need to interact in our complex and diverse society. Throughout the school program attention needs to be given to providing students with opportunities to talk with each other and with the adults in the school community in formal and informal situations.

In classrooms instructors need to create a climate of open communication that encourages students to talk with each other about the activities of the class and about their own interests and experiences. I do not mean organized group discussion of classroom topics but informal conversation among students that is incidental to the tasks of the classroom. Such conversation can occur when students sit in groups in the class and are free to look up and share something they are reading or writing with a neighbor. The model I have in mind is the dinner table conversation that Nancie Atwell suggests in *In the Middle* (1987) or the Sunday breakfast table in my own house where everyone sits over coffee for several hours reading and discussing the *New York Times*. The process of sharing experiences while immersed in individual thinking is aimed not at passing on particular information as much as expressing personal reactions to something we encountered. This talk serves the purpose of "being with" the other as Britton (1982) has pointed out and helps us to get to know each other and see things as the other sees them. After reading and writing across the table from another for a while and listening to the tidbits the other shares, we come to the point where we interrupt to say "You'll love this" or "I can't wait to hear what you think about this." In these exchanges we—that is, all listeners—listen to understand the speaker.

Informal classroom talk is useful to the students not only to listen and come to know other classmates and their thinking better but also to try out their own ideas by "bouncing them off" each other. Allowing a few minutes at some point in the class for students to think aloud with another student about what they are reading or writing and to try out some possible ways of making sense of ideas they are grappling with expands the learning of both listener and speaker. In these experiences students are not relying on each other's comments to provide some needed information they will put to some useful purpose. They may not even be interested in the same topics, but talking together allows them to formulate their thinking with a sympathetic audience.

In my high school the football players used to come into my classroom after school to talk about the team and their prospects for success in the upcoming games. Because I knew little about football but cared a lot about them and their interests, they found me a good audience for trying out their theories on the strengths and weaknesses of the team. They were confident I would listen and ask encouraging questions without ridiculing or contradicting any of their tenuous positions. In those conversations I learned something about football and they probably did solidify their own understandings of the game and the team, but neither was the major effect of those conversations. What really happened was that we all learned more about each other and found ground for relating to each other in ways that were not possible in class.

The example of those conversations with the football players points up another value of social conversation in school: the opportunity to learn each other's language and to find appropriate and effective language for talking with each other. When the football players talked with me they used forms of language very different from those they used in conversations on the same subject with each other; they were consciously using language that respected my age and position in the school and my expectations as their English teacher. Their talk was not only more polite and proper than locker-room talk but also more accessible and more fully explained. And when I tried out terms like "yards rushing" and "quarterback sack," I joined in their laughter at my stilted language, acknowledging their superior knowledge and articulateness in discussing football. We were learning from each other through these conversations, and the most important thing we were learning was how to find a common language comfortable to all of us.

Sometimes in schools teachers purposely plan activities that will put students in social situations that demand certain types of language. The school in which I taught was steeped in tradition and ritual and had a number of occasions annually where students would mingle, formally and informally, with parents, teachers, and other adults from the community. Students served as hosts on open house nights, guiding groups of parents and visitors around the building. They received guests at awards nights each quarter, at National Honor Society inductions, at athletic banquets, at baccalaureate night, and at graduation. They brought their dates through a receiving line at formal dances, introducing guests to the chaperons, exchanging pleasant social comments, and receiving compliments on their finery. The fact that the school had a long tradition of such customs did not mean that students in the school were used to such social interaction, but taking part in those occasions allowed them to learn social language skills through practice and by following the example of more experienced students and caring adults. In my present job I visit schools across New York state, and I often meet students acting as guides or hosting a reception or standing near their art exhibit or science project to respond to visitors' questions. I am always impressed by the ability of young people to adapt their behavior and language to the demands of the social situation, and I am particularly pleased to discover that students who are poised and fluent in social language use come from every grade and every ability level. Skill in social language use seems to be unrelated to academic achievement, and for that reason provides positive school experiences for some struggling students.

I have focused in this discussion on oral-language opportunities. Writing for social interaction is, like Britton's expressive writing (1982), "primarily written-down speech." Notes, journals, invitations, and greetings on handmade cards are all types of writing that use language in the ways I describe here. It is easy to see how opportunities for writing and sending such social messages can be incorporated into every child's schooling.

Vygotsky (1962) long ago argued that all learning, and especially language learning, comes out of social interaction. Providing opportunities in school for language-rich social interaction among students and significant adults is essential to student language development. Those opportunities must be carefully planned to match the diverse needs, interests, and ambitions of our students.

Summary

Four General Exit Outcomes as the Basis for an Integrated Instructional Program

I. Acquire and communicate information and understanding.

II. Respond and contribute to the aesthetic domain.

III. Analyze and evaluate complex positions, issues, and trends.

IV. Interact positively and productively with people from diverse social groups.

Aesthetic Experiences

English Class:

- Organized around student *writing*—both literature (poems, stories, fables, myths, plays, skits, TV scripts, and parodies among others) and literary responses.

- *Reading* literary works of professional writers in the genres in which students are writing and reading the "literature" written in the class. The selection of texts should reflect the values and expectations of the community, the interests and tastes of both teacher and students, and the cultural diversity of the society.

- Classroom *discussion* of literature as essential to establishing a "community of readers." The focus is on discussion as a process of shared meaning making (rather than as turn-taking) that values tentativeness and divergent thinking.

Across the Curriculum:

- Writing aesthetic responses to experiences in content-area classes.

- Both reading literature related to issues, historical periods, and concepts in the content-area curriculum texts of more literary writers in the disciplines for aesthetic experience.

Informational Experiences

English Class:

- Writing to learn (through journals, logs, lists, summaries, and so on) and writing to convey understanding (through essays, reports, research papers, manuals, and précis). The focus is on the message as well as on the form, importance of audience, and writing to join in the academic conversation.
- Reading the writing of other class members, professional writers in the discipline, and the classroom teacher, with a focus on the importance of reading primary texts on a topic.
- Informal classroom conversation to try out and develop ideas, formal opportunities for presenting academic reports orally, and minilessons by teachers.

Across the Curriculum:

- Writing to learn and writing to convey understanding (as in English class) with a primary focus on the content and incidental learning of the discourse conventions of the discipline.
- Reading the works of leading thinkers of the discipline and using dialogue journals as way of exploring readings.
- Classroom talk to explore emerging understanding.

Critical Experiences

English Class:

- Exploratory writing to investigate the relationships among encountered ideas.
- Writing on the same issue from a variety of perspectives.
- Reading primary texts from different perspectives on a common issue.
- Analyzing and criticizing literary texts from multiple critical stances.

Across the Curriculum:

- Using the central concepts of the discipline to evaluate issues and ideas in that discipline, such as concepts of "falsifiability," "validity," "verifiability."
- Reading primary texts by leading thinkers in the discipline who represent different perspectives.

- Writing to investigate differing points of view on questions of interest to the discipline.
- Engaging in informal discussion and formal debate on significant issues.

Social Experiences

In the Classroom:

- Informal conversation with classmates and teachers on topics of interest to class.
- Listening to others as a way of coming to understand them better.
- Working in small groups on projects.
- Sending notes and messages to other members of the class and from the class to others in the community.

Outside of Class:

- Extracurricular activities and projects that involve students in conversation with students from other classes and with adults from the school.
- School assemblies, receptions, and performances that require students to act as hosts or to mingle with guests from the community.
- Sending written invitations, announcements, thank-you notes, and greetings from student organizations to members of the community.

Chapter Seven

High Standards for All Students

Who are the students in our schools today? How do their lives outside school affect their learning in school? What needs, talents, interests, and ambitions do they bring into the classroom? These questions suggest the challenge that we face as educators trying to develop instructional programs that bring all students to high levels of achievement on all the desired learning outcomes. How can teachers bring all students to the same challenging outcomes while respecting the diversity that exists among them?

Cultural Diversity

The "issue" of cultural diversity is, in fact, a complex of several related issues involving questions related to the makeup of the student population, content of the curriculum, and instructional practices. Those elements are closely related but distinct in their implications for the educational program.

Students from Diverse Cultures

Cultural diversity in the student population is increasingly evident in schools across our country. In the early 1980s reports indicated that children from minority cultural groups already made up more than 25 percent of all public school students. Projections indicate that by the year 2000, children from groups designated "minority" will in the aggregate actually make up the majority of the student population in some of our large cities. Today in New York City schools, more than 120 different language communities are represented, and similar numbers are found in schools in California, Florida, Massachusetts, and Texas.

One response of educators to these changing demographics has been to see this diversity as an obstacle—or at least a challenge—to delivering an effective educational program and maintaining high standards of performance. As seen throughout this book, maintaining past standards of performance is not enough in today's increasingly demanding world. Educators must raise standards for all students. As teachers, we cannot expect to be successful in that endeavor if we begin by seeing the cultural knowledge and traditions students bring to class as useless or as an impediment to their learning. Such thinking leads teachers to try to eliminate differences among students by encouraging them to keep their home life and their school life separate and to learn completely new ways of thinking and talking in the classroom. These students are sometimes thought of as "underprepared" for learning, so that teachers try to help them to "catch up" with other students.

Schools are meant to help all students acquire knowledge and ability they lack. Teachers will be more successful in that endeavor by starting from Shirley Brice Heath's conception (1983b) of school as a place that allows students "to capitalize on the skills, values, and knowledge they brought there, and to add on the conceptual structures imparted by the school" (1983, 13). Her view of school does not ignore the fact that some students enter school with more of the knowledge and skills that our society values, but Heath acknowledges that all students bring some knowledge and skills and that the job of education is to build on what all students bring.

Student diversity is a resource for expanding the experiences and language use of all students. The language and life experience every student brings to class enriches the conversation among that community of learners. Students learn, from each other and from the teacher, not only language forms but cultural customs and histories, values and beliefs, and ways of seeing and making sense of the world. In a process classroom where the fundamental mode of learning is dialectical—a conversation among students, teachers, and professional scholars—everyone's knowledge of the world and everyone's ability to see and express their understanding of that world is enriched by the presence of people with diverse backgrounds and perspectives.

Expansion of student repertoires of language forms is an obvious result of classroom conversation among classmates who come from different language communities. I immediately think of the role that schooling plays in helping students acquire the forms of Standard

English. In this land of immigrants, one constant hope of parents for their children's education has been acquisition of the language ability that will give those children access to every area of American society—the goal of Italian, Polish, and Greek immigrants at the turn of this century and a goal for the Haitian, Laotian, Nicaraguan, and Lebanese immigrants today. And rightly so. As seen in earlier chapters, one reality that must be acknowledged is that an ability to use the forms of Standard English is necessary for full participation in many social, political, and economic areas of our society. All students have a right to develop through their school experiences the ability to use those forms as they want and need. Natural conversation with other learners and teachers experienced in Standard English is the surest way to such acquisition.

At the same time classroom dialogue provides opportunity for students to acquire the forms of Standard English, it also provides opportunity for all students to acquire language forms from other cultural groups. Sometimes this is a conscious intention of the program, such as in the encouragement of multilingual learning through mixing students from different language communities within a class. I have visited classes where Spanish-speaking children and children who speak only English were learning together using both Spanish and English. The language facility of the children in their primary language was expanded as they helped their classmates, but at the same time all students were acquiring a second language through their interaction. I think this type of program—and even less-formal opportunities for students to speak with native speakers of other languages—has value for students who speak only English as well as for those who speak English as a second language. In such a context the second language has meaning and application for students far beyond what can be attained through academic study alone.

Student diversity is also a valuable resource in the reading and writing experiences of the class but not because students "represent" the cultures from which they come. Neither individual readers nor individual authors can represent a culture. The contribution of a Vietnamese student to the reading of a text does not give that community of readers the "Vietnamese perspective," but that student's unique cultural experiences may open up aspects of the text not otherwise available. In class discussion students from a variety of cultures can come to understand each other's perspectives, to realize that their way of seeing is not the only possible one, and to recognize the complexity of ideas and issues they are reading about. Those discussions and students' writing about their reading provide evidence of students' progress in a variety of language outcomes. Educators can be confident that the meaning-making ability and language use of all students will be enriched by the presence of a diversity of cultural voices and perspectives.

As teachers, we tend to be generous in our estimations of the oral language and reading competencies of our students, but our evaluations of student writing are much more demanding. Our stricter writing standards are partially due to the demands of mechanical conventions—spelling, punctuation, and capitalization—on writers whose home language is not English or who do not read and write regularly in English outside of school. A command of the conventions of written English is essential to attainment of the desired standards of performance in writing outcomes and may require more direct instruction and constant modeling for students who do not come from highly literate English-speaking homes. However, command of mechanical conventions is only one source of dissatisfaction with student writing. Another source is an expectation that written communication will be more formal in style and diction than oral communication.

While mechanical conventions can be effectively learned through a combination of frequent practice and direct instruction, appropriate style and diction for a variety of writing situations are not so easily learned. In writing for information or critical analysis, adherence to expected standards of style and diction is an important criterion for acceptable performance. To gain that ability students need to be immersed in reading and writing. The opportunity to enter conversation with other thinkers and writers from many disciplines is even more important for students who are not highly literate in English than for students who are, and the selection of appropriate and relevant materials for those students is an especially important responsibility of teachers. Constant immersion of students in reading and writing, dialogue journals, summary writing, and comparisons of different texts are effective techniques for developing both an understanding of ideas and a fluency in language. The cruel irony is that students who most need such literate activities are often denied access to them and are consigned instead to programs focused on direct instruction of grammar and usage and on completion of endless worksheets on isolated skills. Such isolated skill drilling is not producing the desired result of helping students with limited literacy skills to become good writers. Focusing classes instead on the outcomes that teachers really want for students—writing for information and understanding and writing for critical analysis and evaluation at an acceptable adult level—should result in students being engaged in real writing experiences throughout their schooling.

The two other writing outcomes—writing for aesthetic response and expression and writing for social interaction—have different implications. While informational and critical writing are public in intent and, therefore, concerned with expected standards of clarity and sound argument, aesthetic and social writing are highly personal and aim at communicating the individual's uniqueness. Because of the personal nature of that writing, adherence to conventions of Standard English or to expectations of formal usage is not always appropriate or effective, which has always been the case. In the name of poetic license or dialect or (more recently) code switching, teachers have accepted language in imaginative writing that departs purposefully from conventions of written Standard English. The power of writing that captures the real language of real people is evident in the works of Zora Neale Hurston, Alice Walker, Toni Morrison, Toni Cade Bambera, Rudolfo Anaya, Gary Soto, Gloria Anzaldua, Sandra Cisneros, and countless others. Students may not write fictive pieces that demonstrate the same control of language as these writers exhibit, but students' imaginative and social writing will only have power if they find a personal voice and style that conveys their unique personality. Such language is ambiguous and metaphorical and evocative rather than clear and logical and verifiable (Bruner 1986). Therefore, teachers bring different expectations to students' imaginative writing. Not only do instructors expect personal language and style, but they expect that the literary forms students use may very likely come from their cultural heritage as well as from academic experience. Shirley Brice Heath (1983b) described the differences in storytelling conventions between the children from different communities. Another study by Michaels and Cazden (1986) showed not only that the narratives of black and white elementary school children were different in form but also that black and white adults rated more highly narratives composed by children of their own cultural group. These studies remind us that cultural groups have differing conventions for storytelling and imaginative writing, and students will benefit from regular opportunities to read the literature of writers from their own and other cultures as they develop competence as imaginative writers. The need for such opportunities has significant implications for the selection of classroom reading materials.

Multicultural Literature

Selecting literature for classroom study is a highly charged issue. Concerns about ensuring a common (if not a traditional) canon of texts for all students, maintaining recognized standards of literary merit, and preserving a common national identity sometimes make teachers hesitate to introduce new or unfamiliar works. At the same time evidence is mounting that inclusion of all of the cultural voices in our society is crucial to the academic achievement of all students. In the first place, all students must come to know and appreciate the contributions and artistic achievements of people from a wide variety of cultures, an understanding essential to every category of outcome, whether aesthetic, informational, critical, and social. To perform successfully in any of these areas, students need to read widely in the literature of many cultures. In addition, as discussed above, if all students are to achieve the same high standards in the language outcomes, they must have opportunities to read literature that is part of their cultural heritage, literature that may not be familiar to the teacher. How can teachers reconcile those competing pressures?

A desire for a common canon of literature shared by all educated people is understandable. Hirsch's reminder (1987) that people who do not share the common knowledge that makes up the cultural conversation will be excluded from that conversation is hard to ignore, but the implications of that idea need to be examined. Does it mean that teachers can only enter the cultural conversation after studying a vast canon of common literary texts? Is it not also arguable that much cultural knowledge comes from entering the conversation? Many more people recognize references to the trials of Odysseus than have actually read Homer. Our children are more likely to know Tiny Tim and Ebenezer Scrooge through the renditions of Mr. Magoo and Mickey Mouse than from studying Dickens. Certainly it is a rewarding experience for students to read works of literature valued through the generations and to have first-hand experience of texts respected by their teachers and their community, but that experience does not appear to be in jeopardy. Arthur Applebee's (1989) recent study of the literature included in high school programs found that the list of the top ten most frequently taught texts was virtually the same in 1989 as it had been when a similar study was conducted in 1968 (Squire and Applebee 1968). The canon of literature for high school students seems to have been a relatively constant one.

The formation of a literary canon depends on the assumption that standards of literary quality are absolute or, at the most, subject only to minor fluctuation. As discussed above, however, standards of literary quality vary significantly from one culture to another. The works on Applebee's list reflect some of the standards of literary merit that have prevailed in Western literature, and because those standards are so ingrained in teachers' way of thinking, many educators may be reluctant to include works that do not exhibit those same standards. It is possible to expand the selection of literature for classroom reading while also expanding the basis for judging quality.

Two principles might guide teachers in selecting works of significant literary quality. First, instructors need to select texts respected within the culture from which they come. The works on Applebee's list are recognized as classics of the English-speaking world and reflect some of the values of that world. Other cultural groups represented in American society also have canons of works that have gained recognition as masterworks of their culture, and educators have an obligation to our students to find those works in order to provide students with wide-ranging literary experiences. Second, teachers need to familiarize themselves with standards of literary excellence in other cultures. Classroom discussions of the Spider Woman stories from the Native American tradition or Naguib Mahfouz's novels of Egyptian family life should focus on those works as reflections of their own cultures not on the degree to which they reflect European literary conventions. As educators, we need to consider how works reflect the values of their own literary tradition, not try to apply one set of expectations to every text. The process of learning is demanding for teachers trying to know more about multicultural literature at the same time that they are trying to teach it, and an understanding of difference will not come all at once. However, consulting with both teachers and those who are knowledgeable about other cultures (including students and their parents from those cultures) will help us to learn while teaching.

Had teachers but world enough and time, a wide range of works from each cultural group could be included but that is obviously impossible. Educators are forced to select a limited number of works from a few groups, a limitation that seems to account for another trend reported in Applebee's research (1989). His study found that where works by women writers and writers from minority cultures are included in the curriculum they are almost exclusively short works—poems and short stories. The full-length works are predominantly by white English-speaking males. Awareness of that tendency may be the first step toward changing it and including some longer works from minority cultures on reading lists.

How can teachers begin to broaden the literary experiences of all students while maintaining a balance between literature that represents a common cultural tradition and literature that brings new or previously neglected voices into the classroom? There are some approaches that will move toward this goal.

1. Offer some choices for individual or small-group reading of literature. Rather than having the whole class reading Twain's *The Adventures of Huckleberry Finn*, students might be allowed to choose from a list of novels with protagonists from different cultural groups. The list would be determined by the focus of the class at the time—that is, by whether *Huck Finn* is chosen to

represent a particular literary or historical period or a theme (such as interracial brotherhood or moral development), a topic (such as slavery), or a literary element (such as satire, first-person narration, or the picaresque novel). Whatever the focus of study, other works can be found to fit the same focus while offering alternative cultural perspectives and insuring that the cultures of the students are included.

2.   Begin by including voices of cultural groups represented in the class. With the limits of time it is not possible to include all the cultural groups of the American society in the curriculum, but it is essential that all students see themselves and their culture as connected to the classroom experience. It is also important for all students to experience the literature and perspectives of cultural groups in their community even if there are not any students from those groups in the class. Finally, a sampling of works from the broader American society should be included over the years of the students' schooling.

3.   Select works respected within the culture. Finding works the cultural group values may necessitate teachers consulting civic groups or community organizations of those cultural groups as well as published lists of books such as those currently available from the National Council of Teachers of English. The ultimate judgment of the literary merit of a text created within a culture rests with that group.

4.   Balance the images that are presented of the cultural groups. Because teachers assign many works by and about white males, in general instructors should not worry about presenting a biased view of the white male experience. In the case of many cultural groups, however, a balance of images and experiences may be difficult to achieve. Teachers need to select texts that present at least enough variety of experiences to indicate the complexity of the culture and to offset negative images or views of the groups as victims with positive, strong images.

5.   Allow students to select some works for the class. Not every story or poem a student wants to share with the class will be a work of literary merit by any definition, but the opportunity to select a favorite work to be part of the class experience is an important recognition of the students' value and authority in that community of learners.

Instructional Strategies in a Culturally Diverse Classroom

I refer repeatedly throughout this book to the conversation of a community of learners as the dominant mode of learning in an outcomes-based process classroom. That conversation is most important in the classroom in which students bring diverse cultural experiences and languages to the learning. In order to help students make connections between what they know and what they are learning and to help them acquire the language they need to express their expanding understanding, teachers must engage the students in ongoing conversation.

In 1983, Shirley Brice Heath wrote an article based on her research in the southeastern United States. In "A Lot of Talk about Nothing," she describes the classroom of a teacher-researcher who adapted information about the language experiences of the children's homes to develop a curriculum that involved having children spend as much time as possible talking. Children talked with the teacher, with each other, with older and younger students, and with visitors from the community. At the end of the school year, she found most of the children in that class "score above grade level on reading tests, and they are able to write stories, as well as paragraphs of exposition on content areas with which they feel comfortable in their knowledge" (191). The advantage the teacher had in that situation was that Heath's ethnographic study of the the childrens' communities informed the practice of the teacher-researchers and provided cultural information for making connections between the children's homes and their classroom experiences.

Most teachers do not have the assistance of a professional ethnographer as coresearcher to help them understand the cultural patterns of their students. They have to rely on their own knowledge of the students' cultures, and their best sources of such knowledge are the students themselves, members of the parents' organization, and other members of the community the school serves. The teachers must themselves become students of those cultures, students whose main strategy for learning is listening and speaking with all members of the school community.

Shirley Brice Heath's point (1983a) about the importance of talk is corroborated by Mike Rose in *Lives on the Boundary* (1989) with his descriptions of the instructional practices he first came to appreciate as a student and later adopted as a teacher. In the book, Rose describes what he considers to be the best sort of liberal education.

> My teachers modeled critical inquiry and linguistic precision and grace, and they provided various cognitive maps for philosophy and history and literature. They encouraged me to make connections and to enter into conversations—present and past—to see what talking a particular kind of talk would enable me to do with a thorny philosophical problem or a difficult literary text. (Rose 1989, 58)

Rose's experience confirms the importance not only of talk but of the particular type of talk most valuable to students from outside the mainstream culture. Like Heath, he emphasizes the value of talk about talk—conversation that makes explicit the connections between newly encountered concepts or events and what was previously experienced, talk in which the teacher openly models the thinking and language students are trying to acquire.

The work of Rose (1989), Heath (1983), Delpit (1988b), and other researchers suggests several principles for planning instructional strategies for classrooms with culturally diverse student populations.

1. Classroom experiences involve students in many different kinds of talk. Especially important are opportunities to describe experiences, summarize readings, label and classify features of objects or events, and compare and analyze experiences.

2. Much of classroom talk is "talk about talk"—calling attention to features of the thinking and the language use the class is engaged in.

3. Teachers model and explain the kinds of thinking and language use they want students to learn—pointing out connections they are making, questions they are posing, criteria they are using to evaluate something, and the particular language forms they are using.

4. Writing-to-learn activities are a regular part of the daily classroom experience and provide opportunities for students to try out thoughts and language before going public with them.

5. Minilessons focus on direct instruction of particular skills or language conventions and are followed by immediate opportunity for applying the skill in a piece of real writing.

6. Reading, talking about reading, writing about reading, and reading each other's writing are essential to learning the conventions of written English.

7. Every discipline students study in school has its own language conventions. Students learn both the concepts and the language of those disciplines by immersion and guided practice in the ongoing conversation of that discipline.

8. Teachers have an obligation to be ethnographers and to learn as much as they possibly can about the cultural practices of their students. They also need to become more aware of themselves as cultural beings grounded in ways of thinking and acting that may be different from, but not superior to, those of their students.

These instructional practices do not apply only to the language program but to all learning. They are based on the beliefs that language and culture are inseparable and that language and culture are at the heart of all learning. If all students are to achieve the desired learning outcomes, the instructional program must build on the language and cultural patterns students bring into the classroom.

Work Force Preparation

One of the diversities educators are becoming increasingly aware of relates not to students' origins but to their plans for the future. Many teachers have come to recognize that for more than half of all students high school graduation signals entry not into college but into the work force. That recognition prompts the question, How will an outcomes-based education prepare students for work? To address that question I want to start with two assumptions:

1. With few exceptions, all individuals will be part of the work force during most of their adult lives.

2. With few exceptions, all individuals will be involved in some type of higher or continuing education program at some time during their adult lives.

Those assumptions are important for establishing the premise that all individuals need to prepare for both the work force and further study. To consider students as falling into two distinct groups —those bound for the work force and those for continuing study—is to create a false dichotomy. I probably would not get much argument about the first assumption. Whereas in previous generations many students (mostly women) left high school with the expectation that they would not go to work or would work only for a very brief time (until they married and began to raise a family), that is no longer the case. Women have come into almost every area of the work force, and the majority of women will stay in the work force for most of their adult lives except for short periods spent in childcare. Even wealthy and privileged members of our society, who don't depend on jobs for their livelihood, take jobs in business, government, or the professions. America is a country of workers, broadly defined, and preparation for participation in that work force is the right of every student.

The second assumption may not seem as self-evident. When most educators think of education after high school, they are likely to think of full-time attendance at a university, a condition that applies to less than half of American high school graduates. But today continuing education programs proliferate, and people move in and out of them for a wide variety of reasons: to upgrade or diversify job skills, to prepare to reenter the work force after an absence, to retrain for a career change, to acquire skills that will save money on home or auto repairs, to pursue an academic or artistic interest, and to meet other adults with similar interests. Many of the reasons that lead people back to the classroom have to do with the need to become more competitive in a rapidly changing workplace, but certainly that is not the case with all of them. Community colleges and high school extension programs offer courses in art appreciation, botany, home computer use, fiction writing, foreign languages, financial planning, and a myriad of other interests; often people who take these classes are working adults who want to spend their nonworking hours pursuing interests unrelated to their jobs. Even after retirement, people continue to take courses to enrich their lives and meet new people. Senior citizen centers and Elderhostel programs attract large numbers of registrants for diverse educational programs. Lifelong learning is more than just a goal; it is a reality and a necessity.

Work and study—they are not only unavoidable elements of adult life in our society, they are among the elements that give meaning to our lives. Therefore, every student should graduate from high school with the outcomes necessary for full participation in both of those areas of adult life. The division of students into two groups— bound for the workplace or college—with the implication that those two groups need different educational outcomes is inaccurate and detrimental to all students. Ironically, support for the argument that the same set of outcomes is necessary for the work force as for continued study can be found in reports that focus on the demands of the workplace. I say ironically because those reports are often cited as support for proposals of separate programs for work force preparation. The Secretary's Commission on Achieving Necessary Skills (SCANS 1991) first called attention to the fact that "more than half our young people leave school without the knowledge or foundation required to find and hold a good job" (1). Since that report came out much has been written and said about the needs of "the forgotten half." A corollary to the statement that 51 percent of students graduate from high school unprepared for jobs might be that 49 percent graduate from high school with the knowledge and skills needed on the job and, presumably, those students are the same ones prepared for college. Practical experience bears out this assumption. The students who find it easiest to get and keep jobs are often those who are also successful in academic study. The qualities that served them well in school—punctuality, good attendance, interpersonal skills, clear thinking and reasoning, and effective language—are equally important to their success in the workplace. But to argue that the same outcomes achieved by college-bound students are equally important for those going directly into the work force is not to argue that the same programs and learning experiences will meet the needs of all those students. As seen in Chapter 6, a wide variety of rich and challenging programs should be available to allow students to achieve the outcomes through experiences that fit their talents, needs, and ambitions. For students whose ambition is to go immediately into the work force, programs should provide experiences that directly reflect the demands of today's workplace.

The SCANS report and all of the reform reports identify reading, writing, listening, and speaking as basic skills students need for the workplace. But in the SCANS report those basic skills are defined in a rather limited way to "reflect the workplace *contexts* in which they are applied" (4). More helpful to understanding the complex demands of language use necessary for today's students is Naisbitt and Aburdene's *Re-Inventing the Corporation* (1986), in which they argue that an educated, skilled work force for the new information society needs three "new basics"—thinking, learning, and creating. Those basics are directly related to the language outcomes identified here for all students.

Naisbitt's definition of thinking as "the ability to synthesize and make generalizations, to divide into categories, to draw inferences, to distinguish between fact and opinion, [and] to put facts in order to analyze a problem" (126) describes the same kinds of meaning making associated with reading, writing, listening, and speaking for critical analysis and evaluation. The activities considered in Chapter 6 for developing those critical abilities involve students in the kind of thinking that Naisbitt describes. Identifying areas of consonance and dissonance with the opinions of others in discussion groups, keeping a dialogue journal in which to record an ongoing conversation with texts read in class, and writing to discover and to convey one's own opinions, judgments, and analyses are all experiences in thinking and using language critically.

Naisbitt makes a strong case for the relationship of writing to thinking, learning, and creating. He quotes William Zinsser's statement that "clear thinking becomes clear writing: one can't exist without the other," and reasons from that to the conclusion that educators must "strengthen the writing curriculum as an avenue to sharpen thinking." To strengthen the writing curriculum he suggests wider dissemination of the National Writing Project model of teachers and students writing together, increased participation of professional writers in teaching creative writing in the schools, and attention to writing across the curriculum where "The idea," as Naisbitt puts it, "is not to 'teach' writing as such but to use writing to teach all subjects" (1986, 134).

Using writing to teach all subjects applies to occupational subjects as well as to academic subjects. I once visited a technical high school in which students in an animal care program kept logs of the daily diet and activities of each of the animals. They were proud of the technical language they had acquired from consulting manuals for the care of each species and explained to those of us who were visiting any unfamiliar terms we encountered. As we moved through the building, the students showed remarkable poise and authority in explaining distinguishing features of each animal or species, pointing out which ones were compatible with one another and which were not, describing the dispositions and natures of all the creatures, indicating which ones needed special care, and reminding us, ever so gently, of the realities of the food chain when we approached the cage of mice kept conveniently near the python. The engagement of those students in the activities of the animal care program looked much more like a professional business than a typical classroom, and their abilities to read, write, listen, and speak to acquire, interpret, and transmit information and to analyze problems and make judgments and decisions were evident in everything they were doing. The sad fact is that in their school the same engagement and rigorous thinking and language use were not evident in other areas of the curriculum. There was no apparent connection between the knowledge and understanding and language skills students acquired in the animal care program and their other courses. Even in English class there was no evidence of student writing of stories, poems, or even reports that drew on their specialized knowledge and no evidence of opportunities for reading literature and nonfiction related to their interests as a way of broadening their language competence. As a result, many students were not successful in other areas of the school program and most of them had poor scores on traditional measures of verbal ability. Good thinking and language use require constant and connected opportunities to talk and write about important ideas and topics and to build on and expand areas of competence.

Some programs focus on connectedness. At another vocational high school in which the major emphasis was on programs in building trades, students in English class were competing in a local speech contest sponsored by a real estate agency. They had researched building codes and zoning restrictions for their neighborhood and were using their technical knowledge of material and labor costs to argue for the development of low-cost single-family dwellings to replace decaying apartment complexes. In the same school another English class was working with a visiting poet to write poems of their personal experiences. Another alternative high school had a media program that involved students in writing, producing, and editing videos on current issues (gun control in the schools, AIDS prevention, teenage depression). To research material and techniques for their own videos students viewed a number of professional documentaries on similar topics, did research in the library, and interviewed students and community members. They took notes, discussed script ideas, and wrote and edited their scripts. They rehearsed their parts in the video, taped and retaped section after section, directed and critiqued each other's performances, and edited and released the final product. All of this activity took place in an atmosphere that, like the animal care program, was more like a professional business than a typical classroom—and this in a high school for students who could not function successfully in a regular high school. The focus of the program was media technology, but the range of language experiences and learning, as well as the understanding of significant concepts from across the curriculum, was impressive.

In another alternative high school in a large city school system, students who had dropped out of regular programs or returned to school after release from drug rehabilitation programs or prison terms were enrolled in a variety of vocational programs such as health care, technology, and cosmetology. The main text in the eleventh-grade English class was an anthology of writing by former students of the school. Students read and analyzed poems and stories by young people like themselves. They talked about the writing techniques the authors had chosen; they evaluated pieces and compared them to each other and to the work of professional writers. They worked on pieces of their own to be included in future editions, meeting with their peers in writing groups to critique each other's work and offer suggestions for revision and to decide which pieces from the class should be recommended for the anthology. In the same school the journalism class produced a newspaper that contained news articles, feature stories, and editorials on topics of concern to the community. Issues like child care, public health programs, employment counseling, and unemployment regulations figured in the pages of the newspaper as they did in the lives of the students. The classroom teacher was assisted regularly by a professional newspaper reporter who helped students not only with technical concerns of layout and printing but, more importantly, with techniques of information gathering and reporting.

All of these programs were in high schools designed for vocational education, but in every one of them excellent opportunities for thinking, learning, and creating were present. The students were not limited to filling out application forms, composing memos, writing business letters, or filling out order forms or insurance claims—the kinds of writing often associated with the workplace and far too often the extent of the writing opportunities in programs for the noncollege bound. Students were engaged in rigorous and diverse activities that allowed them to develop the knowledge, skills, and attitudes that comprise the desired learning outcomes for all students. These programs illustrate the real value vocational education can have for students and suggest several points about the role of vocational programs in education:

1. As Goodlad argued (1984) in *A Place Called School,* vocational education "is an essential, not merely an elective part of general education. . . . This means that vocational education is for all students, not just an alternative to academic studies for the less academically oriented" (147).

2. The labeling of students as "vocational" or "academic," and the presumption that students in vocational programs will not go on to college are erroneous and a disservice to all students. Not only is a combination of experiences in the arts, sciences, and vocational programs beneficial for all students in high school, but college degree programs are available in all of those areas. Students may choose to pursue a degree in technology, agriculture, or business just as they do in political science, literature, or philosophy.

3. Integration of academic and vocational study is an effective way of helping many at-risk students achieve the desired learning outcomes set for all students. Academic study is made easier when its application to real world situations is apparent. The Grant Commission (1988) in *The Forgotten Half: Pathways to Success for America's Youth and Young Families* endorses "a combination of conceptual study with concrete applications and practical problem-solving" as most effective for many students (129).

4. The goal of vocational programs, according to the interim report of the Grant Commission (1988), is not to prepare students for specific jobs but to motivate students "to acquire the skills and knowledge they need for both work and active citizenship" (51).

The above principles make it clear that access to the same learning outcomes is the right of all students. Whether students are going from high school immediately to the work force or from high school to college, they need the same outcomes for full participation in all aspects of our society. Vocational programs provide an avenue to those outcomes for many students who learn most successfully through practical experience. They are not a substitute for academic study but a way of connecting academics to the world outside of school. They should not limit the future possibilities of students but should open up new possibilities for learning, thinking, and creating.

Students with Handicapping Conditions

Finally, a few words about the group of students who are most likely to be excluded from the expectation that all students can achieve the same high standards of performance on all the desired learning outcomes—those students who are designated as special education students or students with handicapping conditions. Many people who agree in principle with the statements that all children can learn and that there should be the same outcomes and standards for all students exclude children with handicapping conditions. Since 1975 when the Education of Children with Handicapping Conditions Act was passed, the population of students in special education programs has tripled and a great deal of attention has been given to insuring their rights to access to educational programs. Too little of that attention has been directed to insuring that students in special programs attain the full range of learning outcomes expected of all students. Individual Educational Programs (IEPs) are sometimes used to excuse students from particular requirements rather than to find alternative routes to the achievement of those requirements. Part of the problem results from a focus on surface-level skills in establishing requirements rather than on the construction of meaning. In a program such as the one advocated here in which the outcomes refer to the processes of meaning making, students with handicapping conditions can be expected to attain the same outcomes as other students. The performance indicators that describe the particular kind of meaning making involved in each outcome are useful to teachers in insuring that students have experiences to help them attain satisfactory levels of performance on each outcome.

Think about the ability to read of people who are blind. If reading is defined as the recognition and decoding of visual symbols, individuals with limited vision will not be able to attain that outcome. But the discussion of reading in the previous sections says little about perception and decoding of symbols and a great deal about comprehension of meaning, interpretation, analysis, and criticism of texts. All those mental operations can be and are performed by the visually impaired. Through use of braille, audio tapes, or a volunteer reader, the blind have access to written texts. Many of them are highly proficient interpreters and critics of those texts. They make connections between the text and their past literary and life experiences; they recognize significant cultural elements that distinguish the world of the text from their own; they make decisions about the significance and validity of information in the text; and they evaluate ideas in the text from a variety of different perspectives. Those behaviors (and many other similar ones) are all performance indicators used here to define the outcomes for reading, and none of them is dependent upon the ability to see. Blind students can be expected to achieve the same high level of performance on these reading outcomes as those with perfect eyesight.

I start with the example of blind students demonstrating high standards of performance in reading because it is an example that most people would readily agree with. Many readers should be able to name blind people who are excellent readers and scholars. Similar examples can be cited to indicate how individuals with speech or hearing disabilities are able to engage in face-to-face verbal communication through the use of sign language, lip reading, and electronic devices— exhibiting the same ability to interact through language as those with normal speech and hearing. Those examples should remind teachers that in describing language competence educators should be most concerned with indicators of meaning making. Focusing on those indicators would change the way the planning and assessment of educational experiences of students with all types of disabilities, not only those related to physical handicaps but also to the full range of learning disorders—dyslexia, attention deficit, emotional disorders, and hyperactivity. What happens when as instructors we focus on the performance indicators for the language outcomes? Instead of describing their performance in terms of what they cannot do ("Unable to complete assigned tasks") or of errors they make (transposes letters, mistakes b for d) we focus on the kind of thinking we expect them to do. By trying to recognize and develop student ability to "make connections with past literary or life experiences," "make decisions on the significance or validity of information in a text," or "evaluate the ideas in a text from different perspectives," teachers will become more aware of what the student is able to do and can build on, and teachers will also begin to plan classroom experiences that involve students in that kind of meaning making. The principles for planning instructional strategies I described as valuable for teaching students from diverse cultures are equally valuable for students who have learning disorders. Talking to learn, talk about talk, teacher modeling, explanation of thinking and language use, writing to learn, focused minilessons, and constant reading are the surest ways to develop the language competencies of these students.

When Frank Smith (1988) talks about bringing students into the literacy club, his message has special significance for those students who might be excluded from the club through some misguided sense of compassion. Teachers cannot keep some students from full participation in the educational program or reduce expectations for their accomplishment because of a perception that learning is harder for them or takes them longer than the allotted time. These students need the most support and guidance from teachers throughout their school experience; they will not become active members of the literacy club without that support. Instructors may have to find alternative routes to the same outcomes by building on interests students bring into the class from their outside lives—perhaps through the arts, occupational, or sports programs. Instructors may have to allow students more time to attain the outcomes that are the most difficult for them while allowing the students to move ahead in areas they find easier. Instructors may have to rethink notions of what constitutes an educated person, finding the appropriate balance between a common core of content and experiences to which all students are entitled and individualized programs that connect with students' talents, interests, and ambitions. Achieving that balance requires the constant attention of educators. Here are some considerations to keep in mind while balancing these concerns:

1. The broad categories of outcomes—aesthetic, informational, critical, social—define the basic entitlement of all students. There should be provision throughout the educational program for experiences in each of those categories. Educators cannot decide some students are not capable of critical thinking or writing, that others lack the ability for aesthetic expression, or that still others don't need high-level skills for gathering and conveying information.

2. The characteristics of performance that indicate increasing proficiency of performance for the outcomes need explicit attention in classroom experiences of special education students. Teacher modeling and explanation of the *connections* teachers are making, of the necessary *flexibility* in using language for many purposes, and of the *conventions* appropriate in different contexts will make students more conscious of their own thinking and language use and help them to focus on increasing their own *range* and *independence*.

3. Selection of content and learning materials must be guided by the present language and knowledge of the students *and* by the demands of the core curriculum for the school. Whatever common issues, concepts, and ideas form the basis for inquiry and investigation for all other students must be addressed in the programs of special education students, which is not an argument for a common canon of texts but against a "dumbing-down" of the curriculum to exclude some students from grappling with significant content.

4. To the extent possible, school resources should be directed to supporting students with disabilities in the regular program rather than separating them from the rest of the student population. In a process classroom in which learning comes from the interaction of the community of learners, everyone benefits from a diversity of thinking and learning styles in that community.

In a classroom in which students with special needs are part of the community of learners, that community supports their language development by engaging in the desired language use with them. As educators, we can read stories and poems with them and encourage them to tell and write their own stories and poems and share them with the class. We can discuss information students find in their textbooks and other readings and help students to see and explain the connections between what they are reading or hearing and what they know. We can demonstrate how to look at an issue from different perspectives and ask them to do the same thing. We can provide opportunities for them to talk socially with people of different ages, cultures, and classes and point out the language and behavior that is expected for different groups and occasions. Supported practice, constant encouragement, and high expectations will bring students with disabilities into the club of proficient language users. Membership in that club is not only a right but also a need of all of our students. None can be excluded.

Conclusion

Our traditional educational program seems designed to educate the college-bound children of white, middle-class, English-speaking American families, a group of students that will soon make up a minority population within the total school population. The majority of students today are likely to fall into one or more category usually referred to as members of some special interest group, such as students from nonwhite and/or non-English- speaking cultures, students going directly from high school to the workplace, and students in special education programs. Our educational system must insure that those students have the opportunity to achieve the learning outcomes to which they are entitled.

The only constant in education today is change. We cannot as educators hope to get the system right once for all future times. As we try to determine what outcomes are necessary for today's students, what educational programs will bring all students to those outcomes, and what standards of performance will guarantee our graduates full participation in the global society, we must keep in mind that today's answers will be inadequate for tomorrow's challenges. As soon as we can agree on the outcomes and standards for language use today, we need to revisit them to see how they should be redefined and modified as tomorrow approaches and the demands on our graduates change.

The process of defining language standards is an evolutionary one. We must be ready at every stage to put away standards we have just agreed on and embrace standards that reflect the demands of a new day. We should keep in mind Eliot's words:

> "For last year's words belong to last year's language
> And next year's words await another voice."

We have our standards, but they are always in process.

Appendix

Revised Draft of Outcomes with Eight Levels of Performance

Levels of Performance

Level 1—beginning elementary

Level 2—independent elementary

Level 3—dependent intermediate

Level 4—independent intermediate

Level 5—minimal adult competency

Level 6—mature proficiency

Level 7—exceptional proficiency

Level 8—standard-setting professional

Reading for Aesthetic Response

Meaning: The individual can enjoy and appreciate texts, relate texts to self, and respond sensitively to texts with diverse social, historical, and cultural dimensions.

1. The individual will with direction and guidance

   - read and enjoy children's texts from a limited range of genres and subjects.
   - relate events in those texts to his/her own life.
   - read with guidance children's literature set in different cultures, recognize similarities between those cultures and his/her own culture, and appreciate the contributions of those cultures when they are pointed out.
   - appreciate the language and the story structure.

2. The individual will independently

   - read and enjoy children's texts from a wide range of genres and subjects.
   - relate events and ideas from those texts to his/her own life.
   - select and read children's literature set in different cultures, recognize similarities between those cultures and his/her own culture, and appreciate the contributions of those cultures when they are pointed out.
   - recognize and explain the effects of language and story structure.

3. The individual will with direction and guidance

   - read and enjoy young adult texts from a limited range of genres and subjects.
   - recognize aspects of young adult texts that are relevant to his/her own life.
   - read with guidance young adult literature set in different cultures, recognize common human experiences in that literature, and appreciate the contributions of those cultures when those common experiences and specific contributions are pointed out.
   - appreciate the ways that language and text structure evoke a response.

4. The individual will independently

   - read and enjoy young adult texts from a wide range of genres and subjects.
   - recognize aspects of young adult texts that are relevant to his/her own life.

- select and read young adult literature set in different cultures, recognize common human experiences in that literature, and appreciate the contributions of those cultures when those common human experiences and specific contributions are pointed out.
- recognize and explain those elements in texts that prompt a personal response.

5. The individual will

- read and enjoy texts from a limited range of genres and subjects.
- recognize aspects of texts that are relevant to his/her own life.
- recognize common human experiences in literature of one's own and other cultures and appreciate the contributions of those cultures when those common experiences and specific contributions are pointed out.
- appreciate the ways that language and text structure evoke a response.

6. The individual will

- read and enjoy complex texts in all genres on a wide range of subjects.
- explain his/her responses with reference to prior literary and life experiences.
- recognize the common human experiences in literature of one's own and other cultures and appreciate the uniqueness of those cultures.
- recognize and explain those elements in texts that prompt a personal response.

7. The individual will

- read selectively for his/her own purposes in complex texts of all genres on a wide range of subjects.
- select certain aspects of his/her past experiences that contribute most to understanding and explain the feelings, attitudes, and ideas evoked by the text.
- recognize the specific experiences and values that distinguish one culture from another; read not only to learn "about" but also to learn "from" people of other cultures.
- recognize traditional forms and conventions for the literary genres and focus attention on those textual elements that produce the most satisfactory response; explain the contributions of those elements to the emerging meaning of the literary text.

8. The individual will

- find personal meaning in any text in English.

- synthesize past experiences and prior knowledge with textual elements in what appears to be an automatic recognition and rejection of irrelevant associations.

- recognize that every reading experience involves two sets of values and cultural contexts, the reader's and the author's; recognize the tensions that result from the differences in those contexts and reflect on those tensions to understand his/her own response.

- select and synthesize textual elements to develop a response, actively revising and resynthesizing as he/she reads.

Reading For Information and Understanding

Meaning: The individual can collect data, facts, or ideas; discover relationships, concepts, or generalizations; and can use knowledge generated from text.

1. The individual will with direction and guidance

- acquire information from children's reference books, magazines, elementary textbooks, and other informational material for children on a limited range of subjects.

- gather information from a few simple forms with guidance and use the information for a given purpose.

- recognize some relationships among information from a limited variety of sources of informational material for children, understand common elements in categories, and make some generalizations with direction.

- use given strategies to collect and use information with direction.

2. The individual will independently

- acquire information from children's reference books, magazines, elementary textbooks, and other informational material for children on a wide range of subjects.

- gather information independently from a selection of simple forms and use the information for his/her own purposes.

- discover some relationships among information from a wide variety of sources of informational material for children, understand common elements in categories, and make some generalizations with minimal direction.

- use given strategies to collect and use information independently.

3. The individual will with direction and guidance

- acquire information from general reference materials, teen magazines, high school textbooks, and books for young adults on a limited range of subjects.

- gather information from a limited variety of traditional forms with guidance and use the information for specific prescribed purposes.

- recognize some relationships among information from a limited variety of sources of informational material for young adults, understand underlying concepts, and make some generalizations with direction.

- apply given strategies for collecting and using information from texts with direction.

4. The individual will independently

- acquire information from general reference materials, teen magazines, high school textbooks, and books for young adults on a wide range of subjects.

- gather information independently from a limited variety of traditional forms and use the information for his/her own purposes.

- discover some relationships among information from a wide variety of sources of informational material for young adults, perceive underlying concepts, and make some generalizations with minimal direction.

- select and apply appropriate traditional strategies for collecting and using information from texts.

5. The individual will

- acquire information from printed material on a limited range of subjects.

- gather information presented in a limited variety of forms and use the information for specific prescribed purposes.

- discover some relationships among information from a limited variety of sources, perceive underlying concepts, and make some generalizations with direction.

- apply new information to the immediate context but is limited in ability to apply information and understanding from one context in another context.

- use conventional strategies for collecting and using information from texts as directed.

6. The individual will

- acquire information from printed material on a wide range of subjects and make distinctions about the relative significance of specific data, facts, or ideas.

- gather information presented in a wide variety of forms and use that information for a wide range of purposes.

- discover some relationships among information from a variety of sources, perceive underlying concepts, and make generalizations with minimal direction.

- apply information and understanding from one context to a limited range of other contexts.

- select and apply appropriate strategies for collecting and using information from texts.

7. The individual will

- acquire information from complex and sophisticated printed material on a wide variety of subjects and support decisions about relative significance of specific data, facts, or ideas.

- make selective use of a wide variety of forms to gather information for his/her own purposes.

- discover relationships among information from a variety of sources, perceive underlying concepts, and make generalizations without direction.

- apply information and understanding from one context to a wide range of other contexts.

- make judgments about the effectiveness of conventional strategies for acquiring information and adapt those strategies as appropriate.

8. The individual will

- make purposeful selection of desired information from complex and sophisticated material on a wide variety of subjects.

- make creative use of wide variety of forms to gather information for his/her own purposes.

- show insight and originality in discovering relationships among information from a variety of sources, in perceiving underlying concepts, and in making generalizations independently.

- apply information and understanding from one context to a wide range of other contexts and make judgments about the validity and value of such applications.

- make creative use of conventional and individual strategies for acquiring information.

Reading for Critical Analysis and Evaluation

Meaning: The individual can use personal and/or objective criteria to form opinions or to make judgments about ideas and information in written texts.

1. The individual will with direction and guidance

   - use personal or objective criteria to assess the ideas, information, and language in children's texts on a limited range of subjects.
   - analyze children's texts in a limited variety of genres using criteria that reflect personal taste and perspective and objective criteria that direct attention to particular textual elements appropriate to the genre.
   - apply criteria with direction.

2. The individual will independently

   - use personal or objective criteria to assess the ideas, information, and language in children's texts on a wide range of subjects.
   - analyze children's texts from a wide variety of genres using personally selected criteria that reflect personal values, knowledge of a few particular textual elements appropriate to the genre, and knowledge of the subject and the purpose for reading.
   - apply some criteria without direction.

3. The individual will with direction and guidance

   - use personal or objective criteria to assess the ideas, information, and language in young adult texts on a limited range of subjects.
   - analyze young adult texts in a limited variety of genres using criteria that reflect personal perspective and provided criteria that direct attention to particular textual elements appropriate to the genre.
   - apply those criteria when directed.

4. The individual will independently

   - use personal or objective criteria to assess the ideas, information, and language in young adult texts on a wide range of subjects.
   - analyze young adult texts from a wide variety of genres using personally selected criteria that reflect personal perspective,

knowledge of a few particular textual elements appropriate to the genre, and knowledge of the subject and the purpose for reading.

- apply the criteria without direction.

5. The individual will

- use personal or objective criteria to assess the ideas, information, and language in texts on a limited range of subjects.
- analyze texts in a limited variety of genres using criteria that reflect personal perspective and knowledge of textual elements.
- apply those criteria when directed.

6. The individual will

- use personal and objective criteria to assess the ideas, information, and language in texts on a wide range of subjects.
- analyze texts from a wide variety of genres selecting criteria that reflect personal perspective and knowledge of textual elements and are appropriate to the subject and purpose for reading.
- apply the criteria without direction.

7. The individual will

- formulate criteria, both personal and objective, to assess the ideas, information, and language in texts on a wide range of subjects.
- analyze texts from all genres using criteria from a number of given critical and cultural perspectives, selecting perspectives appropriate to the subject and the purpose for reading.
- synthesize and apply criteria derived from different critical and cultural perspectives.

8. The individual will

- recognize the underlying assumptions and values by which he/she assesses the ideas, information, and language in texts from a wide range of subjects.
- tolerate and accommodate a wide range of analyses of a text based on diverse critical and cultural perspectives.
- formulate a unique analysis of a text that yields a new insight or understanding of the text.

Writing for Aesthetic Response and Expression

Meaning: The individual can use written language to express self and to entertain.

1. The individual will with direction and guidance

   - write to express personal feelings about and reactions to a limited range of simple stories, poems, songs, and performances.
   - use simple written language to express a personal response that relates events from stories or personal experiences to his/her own life.
   - use simple language to write simple stories, poems, or songs.

2. The individual will independently

   - write to express personal feelings about and reactions to a wide range of simple stories, poems, songs, and performances.
   - use simple written language to express a personal response that relates events from stories and personal experience to his/her own life.
   - use simple language to write a variety of simple stories, poems, and songs.

3. The individual will with direction and guidance

   - write to express personal feelings about and reactions to a limited range of well-known artistic achievements from his/her own and other cultures.
   - use appropriate written language to express a personal response that explores the connections between the literary text or other artistic experience and his/her own life, and that identifies aspects of common human experience as well as distinct culture features.
   - use written language for artistic expression in a range of genres.

4. The individual will independently

   - write to express personal thoughts and feelings in response to well known artistic achievements from his/her own or other cultures.
   - use appropriate written language to express a personal response that explores the connections between the literary text or other artistic experience and his/her own life, and that identifies aspects of common human experience as well as distinct cultural features.

- use written language effectively for artistic expression in a range of genres with a noticeable sense of personal voice.

5. The individual will

- write in a variety of forms for investigating and expressing personal feelings, attitudes, and ideas related to a limited range of subjects.
- find words and structures that allow personal exploration and refinement of thinking through writing.
- use language effectively to communicate personal feelings, attitudes, and ideas to a variety of audiences, relying on models and direction.
- when appropriate use Standard English.

6. The individual will

- select and use appropriate forms for investigating and expressing feelings, attitudes, and ideas related to a wide range of subjects.
- select words and structures to capture for another time the feelings, attitudes, and ideas evoked by a particular experience.
- use metaphorical/figurative or analytic/scientific language as appropriate to communicate feelings, attitudes, or ideas to a variety of audiences.
- when appropriate use Standard English skillfully.

7. The individual will

- draw on a wide variety of forms to investigate and express feelings, attitudes, and ideas related to a wide range of complex subjects.
- make creative and effective use of words and structures to form images or explanations of experiences and to suggest interpretations and connections.
- use metaphorical/figurative or analytic/scientific language to communicate experiences to a variety of audiences in a way that re-creates the particular feelings, attitudes, and ideas of the writer.
- manipulate the conventions of Standard English for effect.

8. The individual will

- devise new forms for writing to explore and express feelings, attitudes, and ideas related to a wide range of complex subjects.

- synthesize new and prior experiences through effective use of language and structures to come to a new understanding of self and the experiences.

- use metaphorical/figurative or analytic/scientific language to distinguish feelings, attitudes, and ideas in a specific context from those in other contexts and to convey that distinction to a variety of audiences.

- depart purposefully from the conventions of Standard English.

Writing for Social Interaction

Meaning: The individual can use all the forms of writing to communicate in everyday interpersonal situations.

1. The individual will with direction and guidance

- write notes and cards to friends and relatives to keep in touch with people at a distance and to commemorate special occasions.

- communicate personal feelings and experiences to peers and significant adults in personal language.

2. The individual will independently

- write notes and cards to friends and relatives to keep in touch with people at a distance and to commemorate special occasions.

- communicate personal feelings and experiences to peers and significant adults in personal language.

3. The individual will with direction and guidance

- use a variety of written forms (letters, notes, cards, simple verses, skits, song lyrics, etc.) to keep in touch with friends and relatives at a distance and to commemorate special occasions in the lives of family, friends, and acquaintances from the community.

- communicate personal feelings and experiences to friends, family, and acquaintances from the community in personal language appropriate to the relationship and occasion.

4. The individual will independently

- use a variety of written forms to keep in touch with friends and relatives at a distance and to commemorate special occasions in the lives of family, friends, and acquaintances from the community.

- communicate personal feelings and experiences to friends, family, and acquaintances from the community in personal language appropriate to the relationship and the occasion.

5. The individual will

- write in a limited variety of forms on a limited range of subjects for a variety of social purposes and audiences.
- make necessary connections among message, audience, and context.
- use conventions of form and organizational patterns appropriate to the purpose and audience with direction.
- make appropriate use of grammatical structures and of a varied and appropriate vocabulary.
- use Standard Written English.

6. The individual will

- write effectively in a variety of forms on a wide range of subjects for a variety of social purposes and audiences.
- make effective connections among message, audience, and context.
- make an assured and selective use of the conventions of form and organizational patterns appropriate to purpose and audience.
- make use of a wide range of grammatical structures and of an extensive vocabulary to achieve an individual style.
- use Standard Written English skillfully.

7. The individual will

- write on complex and sophisticated subjects using traditional forms creatively for a wide variety of social purposes and audiences.
- make insightful connections among message, audience, and context.
- show originality in adapting conventions of form and organizational patterns to particular purpose and audience.
- achieve pleasing or striking effects by the selective use of grammatical structures and vocabulary.
- manipulate the conventions of Standard Written English for effect.

8. The individual will

- write with authority on a wide range of complex and sophisticated subjects, devising new forms for writing for particular social purposes, incorporating elements of traditional forms where desirable, and making judgments about the relative effectiveness of different forms.
- make original connections among message, audience, and context.
- design and implement new protocols for social correspondence.
- use grammatical structures and vocabulary creatively.
- depart purposefully from the conventions of Standard Written English.

Writing for Information and Understanding

Meaning: The individual can write to acquire, interpret, apply, and transmit information.

1. The individual will with direction and guidance

- present a clear understanding of information on familiar topics.
- use a few simple written forms (e.g., lists, paragraphs, charts) to present information to peers and significant adults.
- indicate through order of presentation and verbal cues the relative importance of information presented.
- demonstrate an awareness of basic writing conventions (spelling, punctuation, and capitalization) and some sentence structures that are different from those of oral language.

2. The individual will independently

- present a clear understanding of information on familiar topics.
- use a few simple written forms (e.g., lists, paragraphs, charts) to present information to peers and significant adults.
- indicate through order of presentation and verbal cues the relative importance of information presented.
- demonstrate an awareness of basic writing conventions (spelling, punctuation, and capitalization) and some sentence structures that are different from those of oral language.

3. The individual will with direction and guidance

- present a clear understanding of information from a variety of sources on relevant personal and academic topics.

- use a variety of written forms (e.g., essays, news articles, reports, outlines, business letters, prepared speeches) to present a clear understanding of information to general audiences.
- establish the relationships among the pieces of information through rhetorical patterns and verbal cues.
- make appropriate use of grammatical constructions and vocabulary.
- use Standard English.

4. The individual will independently

- present a clear understanding of information from a variety of sources on relevant personal and academic topics.
- use a variety of written forms (e.g., essays, news articles, reports, outlines, business letters, prepared speeches) to present a clear understanding of information to general audiences.
- establish the relationships among the pieces of information through rhetorical patterns and verbal cues.
- make assured and selective use of grammatical constructions and vocabulary.
- use Standard English.

5. The individual will

- present essential information clearly and coherently on a limited range of subjects.
- use a limited variety of forms to achieve a given purpose for a particular audience.
- differentiate the relative significance of information and make generalizations and draw conclusions based on that information.
- use conventions of form and organizational patterns appropriate to the subject, purpose, and audience.
- make appropriate use of a range of grammatical constructions and of a varied and appropriate vocabulary.
- use Standard English.

6. The individual will

- present information clearly, coherently, and effectively on a wide range of subjects.
- draw on a wide range of forms to accomplish intended purposes for a variety of audiences.

- support decisions about the relative significance of information with appropriate argument and synthesize information from a variety of sources to make generalizations and draw conclusions.
- make an assured and selective use of the conventions of form and organizational patterns appropriate to the subject, purpose, and audience.
- make use of a wide range of grammatical constructions and vocabulary to achieve an individual style.
- use Standard English skillfully.

7. The individual will

- present complex and sophisticated information clearly and coherently on a wide range of topics.
- make selective and effective use of a wide variety of forms for a wide variety of purposes and audiences.
- present information selectively, making independent decisions about focus, significance, subordination, and exclusion, and draw on a wide range of knowledge to support generalizations and conclusions.
- show originality in adapting conventions of form and organizational patterns to subject, purpose, and audience.
- achieve pleasing or striking effects by the selective use of grammatical constructions and vocabulary.
- manipulate the conventions of Standard English for effect.

8. The individual will

- demonstrate in writing a depth of understanding of subject matter from across a broad range of disciplines.
- present information in unique and effective ways through creative use of forms for a wide variety of purposes and audiences.
- recognize and articulate the values and assumptions underlying decisions about significance, central focus, subordination, and exclusion.
- design and implement protocols that cause readers to perceive information in new and intended ways.
- use grammatical structures and vocabulary creatively while maintaining control of the purpose of the writing.
- depart purposefully from the conventions of Standard English.

Writing for Critical Analysis and Evaluation

Meaning: The individual can use personal or objective criteria to express opinions and make judgments about issues, ideas, and experiences.

1. The individual will with direction and guidance

   - present simple analyses and judgments of a limited range of familiar issues, ideas, and experiences according to given criteria.
   - use a few simple written forms to present opinions.
   - make decisions about the validity and value of particular arguments and indicate those decisions through verbal cues.
   - demonstrate an awareness of basic writing conventions (spelling, punctuation, and capitalization) and some sentence structures that are different from those of oral language.

2. The individual will independently

   - present simple analyses and judgments of a limited range of familiar issues, ideas, and experiences according to given criteria.
   - use a few simple forms (letters, advertisements, journal entries) to present opinions.
   - make decisions about the validity and value of particular arguments and indicate those decisions through verbal cues.
   - demonstrate an awareness of basic writing conventions (spelling, punctuation, and capitalization) and some sentence structures that are different from those of oral language.

3. The individual will with direction and guidance

   - present clear analyses and judgments of a limited range of current issues, ideas, and experiences according to given or self-selected criteria.
   - use a variety of forms to present opinions for audiences of peers or significant adults.
   - make decisions about the validity and value of particular arguments from a specific perspective and indicate those decisions through rhetorical patterns and verbal cues.
   - make appropriate use of grammatical constructions and vocabulary.
   - use Standard English.

4. The individual will independently

- present clear analyses and judgments of a limited range of current issues, ideas, and experiences according to given or self-selected criteria.
- use a variety of forms to present opinions for audiences of peers or significant adults.
- make decisions about the validity and value of particular arguments from a specific perspective and indicate those decisions through rhetorical patterns and verbal cues.
- make assured and selective use of grammatical constructions and vocabulary.
- use Standard English.

5. The individual will

- analyze and evaluate issues and ideas from a limited range of subject areas.
- write in a limited variety of forms to achieve a given purpose for a particular audience.
- assign significance to particular facts and ideas and evaluate the validity and applicability of those facts and ideas using given or self-selected criteria.
- use conventions of form and organizational patterns appropriate to subject, purpose, and audience.
- make appropriate use of a wide range of grammatical constructions and of a varied and appropriate vocabulary.
- use Standard English.

6. The individual will

- analyze and evaluate issues and ideas from·a wide range of subject areas, making appropriate connections among subject areas.
- draw on a wide range of forms to accomplish intended purposes for a variety of audiences.
- articulate the assumptions and values on which opinions and judgments are based and examine those assumptions and values from a variety of perspectives.
- make an assured and selective use of the conventions of form and organizational patterns appropriate to subject, purpose, and audience.
- make use of a wide range of grammatical constructions and vocabulary to achieve an individual style.
- use Standard English skillfully.

7. The individual will

- synthesize complex understandings from a variety of subject areas to formulate criteria for analyzing a wide variety of issues and ideas.
- make selective and effective use of a wide variety of forms for a wide variety of purposes and audiences.
- recognize the assumptions and values underlying a wide variety of issues and perspectives and articulate a personal position that acknowledges areas of agreement and disagreement with other perspectives.
- demonstrate originality in adapting conventions of form and organizational patterns to subject, purpose, and audience.
- achieve pleasing or striking effects by the selective use of grammatical structures and vocabulary.
- manipulate the conventions of Standard English for effect.

8. The individual will

- make judgments about the relative validity and applicability of particular criteria for analyzing issues and ideas from a wide variety of subject areas.
- present analyses and evaluations in unique and effective ways through creative use of forms for a wide variety of purposes and audiences.
- recognize and accept a number of valid perspectives on a wide variety of issues and ideas and make informed selection of an appropriate perspective based on the content.
- demonstrate creativity and insight in designing and implementing protocols that establish the validity of the analyses and evaluations.
- use grammatical structures and vocabulary creatively.
- depart purposefully from conventions of Standard English.

Listening and Speaking for
Aesthetic Response and Expression

Meaning: The individual can enjoy and appreciate oral presentations and can use oral language to express self and to entertain.

1. The individual will with direction and guidance

- understand and respond to presentations of simple stories, poems, and songs.

- express in simple language a personal response that relates the story to his/her own life.
- use simple language to tell stories and to present stories, poems, and songs for an audience.

2. The individual will independently

- understand and respond to presentations of a wide range of simple stories, poems and songs.
- express in simple language a personal response that relates that literature to his/her own life.
- use simple language effectively to tell stories and to present stories, poems, and songs for a variety of audiences.

3. The individual will with direction and guidance

- understand and respond to presentations of a limited range of dramatic performances and other oral presentations on familiar themes and topics.
- use appropriate language to express a personal response that makes clear the connection between his/her personal experience and the presentation.
- use language effectively for oral presentation of an artistic or entertaining nature for an audience.

4. The individual will independently

- understand and respond to presentations of a wide range of dramatic performances and other oral presentations on familiar themes and topics.
- use appropriate language to express a personal response that makes clear the connection between his/her personal experience and the presentation.
- use language effectively for oral presentations of an artistic or entertaining nature for a variety of audiences.

5. The individual will

- recognize and express feelings, attitudes, and ideas evoked by oral presentations on a limited range of subjects and in a limited variety of formats.
- explain responses with reference to personal experiences and values when directed by someone.
- evoke the response of an audience by presenting personal experiences or stories in effective and appropriate language, observing appropriate conventions.

6. The individual will

- recognize and express feelings, attitudes, and ideas evoked by oral presentations on a wide range of subjects and in a wide variety of formats.
- explain responses with reference to personal experiences and values and with reference to significant elements of the presentation.
- evoke a range of responses from a variety of audiences by presenting personal experiences or stories through effective use of language, gesture, tone, and other presentational strategies.

7. The individual will

- recognize and express feelings, attitudes, and ideas evoked by complex oral presentations on a wide range of subjects and in a wide variety of formats.
- explain responses in a manner which distinguishes between those based on personal associations and those elicited by elements of the presentation and which connects the responses with universal human experiences.
- use language and presentational strategies creatively and effectively to evoke a wide range of responses in audiences.

8. The individual will

- recognize and express complex and ambiguous feelings, attitudes, and ideas evoked by complex oral presentations on a wide range of subjects and in a wide variety of formats.
- explain responses in a way that synthesizes elements of the presentation and personal associations and recognizes the universal elements in the response as well as the factors which make every response unique.
- influence the thinking and behavior of audiences in a wide variety of presentations through use of original and effective language and presentational strategies.

Listening and Speaking for Social Interaction

Meaning: The individual can communicate through spoken language in everyday interpersonal situations.

1. The individual will with direction and guidance

- engage in discussion of familiar topics with peers and significant adults.

- listen when required to listen and speak when required to speak.
- listen attentively to others and respond appropriately.
- follow conventions of behavior appropriate to the group.
- use language appropriate to the group.

2. The individual will independently

- engage in discussions of a wide range of familiar topics with peers and significant adults.
- recognize when it is appropriate to listen and when to speak.
- listen attentively to others and respond appropriately.
- determine and follow the conventions of behavior appropriate to the group.
- use language appropriate to the group.

3. The individual will with direction and guidance

- engage in discussion of a few topics of general interest with peers and adults in the community.
- participate in group conversation to an extent appropriate to his/her relative experience and standing in the group.
- listen sensitively and attentively to others and contribute appropriately to the conversation.
- follow the conventions of behavior appropriate to the group in school, family, and neighborhood.
- use language appropriate to the group and its purpose.

4. The individual will independently

- engage in discussion of a range of topics of general interest with peers and adults in the community.
- participate in group conversation to an extent appropriate to his/her relative experience and standing in the group.
- listen sensitively and attentively to others and contribute appropriately to the conversation.
- recognize and follow the conventions of behavior appropriate to groups in school, family, and neighborhood.
- use language appropriate to the group and its purpose.

5. The individual will

- engage in conversation or discussion on a limited range of subjects with a limited range of groups or individuals for a variety of purposes.

- assume an assigned role within a group.
- express personal thoughts and feelings and attend to the thoughts and feelings of others.
- recognize and practice as directed the conventions of behavior (e.g., social etiquette, established procedures, and rules or order) appropriate to a limited range of social groups.
- use the level of language appropriate to a particular group and role.

6. The individual will

- engage in conversation or discussion on a wide range of subjects with a wide variety of groups or individuals for a wide variety of purposes.
- select and assume an appropriate role within a group.
- express personal thoughts and feelings and accept and respond to the thoughts and feelings of others.
- recognize and practice without direction the conventions of behavior appropriate to a wide range of social groups from the local community.
- use in precise and articulate manner the level of language and vocabulary appropriate to a wide variety of groups and roles.

7. The individual will

- engage in conversation or discussion on complex and sophisticated topics with a wide variety of groups or individuals for a wide variety of purposes.
- assume a variety of roles as dictated by the needs of the group.
- influence others from diverse cultural groups through effective expression of thoughts and feelings and respond sensitively to the verbal and nonverbal signals of others.
- understand and practice conventions of behavior appropriate to diverse cultural groups from all segments of American society.
- vary language and vocabulary to achieve a desired effect within a group.

8. the individual will

- engage in conversation or discussion of considerable depth on complex and sophisticated topics with a wide variety of groups for a wide variety of purposes.
- perceive the appropriate role for himself/herself within a group and perform that role independently.

- promote group harmony among diverse people of all cultural groups through the expression of his/her own thoughts and feelings and through empathetic response to other group members.
- understand and practice conventions of behavior appropriate to diverse cultural groups from throughout the global community.
- use language creatively to achieve an intended effect within a group.

Listening and Speaking for Information and Understanding

Meaning: The individual can acquire, interpret, apply, and transmit information through oral language.

1. The individual will with direction and guidance

    - acquire information on familiar topics from simple oral presentations.
    - draw on prior knowledge to understand the significance of orally presented information.
    - make appropriate use of new information to accomplish a given task or add to understanding.
    - present orally a clear understanding of information for an audience.

2. The individual will independently

    - acquire information on a wide range of familiar topics from simple oral presentations.
    - draw on prior knowledge to understand the significance of orally presented information.
    - make selective and appropriate use of new information to accomplish a task or add to understanding.
    - present orally a clear understanding of information for a variety of audiences.

3. The individual will with direction and guidance

    - acquire and recall information on a limited range of relevant personal and academic topics from a limited range of oral presentations designed for a general audience.
    - determine the significance of orally presented information to his/her own personal or academic purposes.

- make selective and appropriate use of new information for given purposes.

- present orally a clear understanding of appropriate academic and personal topics in language appropriate for a variety of contexts and audiences.

4. The individual will independently

- acquire and recall information on a wide range of relevant personal and academic topics from a limited range of oral presentations designed for a general audience.

- determine the relative significance of orally presented information to his/her own personal or academic purposes.

- make selective and appropriate use of new information for self-determined purposes.

- present orally a clear understanding of appropriate academic and personal topics in language appropriate for a variety of contexts and audiences.

5. The individual will

- obtain and recall as required essential information on a limited range of subjects from formal and informal oral communications.

- recognize the significance of new information, make generalizations, and draw conclusions based on new information with direction.

- apply new information to the immediate context but is limited in ability to apply information and understanding from one context in a different context.

- present information clearly and logically on a limited range of subjects in a limited variety of speaking situations using language appropriate to the topic and audience and adhering to established conventions.

6. The individual will

- obtain and recall as required essential information on a wide range of subjects from oral communications, both formal and informal.

- make decisions about the relative significance of new information, make generalizations, and draw conclusions based on new information with minimal direction.

- apply information and understanding from one context to a limited range of new contexts.

- present information clearly and logically on a wide range of subjects in a variety of speaking situations using language appropriate to the topic and audience and making effective application of established rules and conventions.

7. The individual will

- obtain for self-determined purposes complex and sophisticated information from oral communications both formal and informal.
- make decisions about the relative significance of new information, make generalizations, and draw conclusions independently.
- apply information and understanding from one context to a wide range of new contexts.
- select, organize, and present information clearly and logically in a wide variety of speaking situations using language and conventions appropriate to the topic, audience, and context.

8. The individual will

- synthesize for self-determined purposes complex and sophisticated information on a wide range of subjects from oral communications ranging from informal to highly technical or specialized.
- show insight and originality in making decisions about the relative significance of new information, in making generalizations, and in drawing conclusions independently.
- apply information and understanding from one context to a wide range of new contexts and make judgments about the validity and value of such applications.
- show insight and originality in presenting complex and sophisticated understanding of information from a wide range of subjects and can make spontaneous judgments about the most effective ways of presenting information in the immediate context.

Listening and Speaking for Critical Analysis and Evaluation

Meaning: The individual can evaluate and generate information and ideas according to personal and/or objective criteria.

1. The individual will with direction and guidance

- use personal criteria and given objective criteria to assess the content and delivery of simple oral presentations on familiar topics.

- express orally simple analyses and judgments of a limited range of familiar issues, ideas, and experiences according to specific given criteria.

- use simple but clear language that reflects control of some fundamental language conventions.

- monitor and adjust his/her own oral presentations to conform to given criteria for acceptable performance.

2. The individual will independently

- use personal criteria and given objective criteria to assess the content and delivery of a wide range of simple oral presentations on familiar topics.

- express orally simple analyses and judgments of a wide range of familiar issues, ideas, and experiences according to specific given criteria.

- use simple but clear language that reflects control of some fundamental language conventions.

- monitor and adjust his/her own oral presentations to conform to given criteria for acceptable performance.

3. The individual will with direction and guidance

- use personal and objective criteria to assess the content, organization, and delivery of oral presentations designed for a general audience on relevant personal and academic topics.

- express orally clear analyses and judgments of a limited range of issues, ideas, and experiences of general interest according to specific given criteria.

- use clear language that reflects control of language conventions appropriate to a limited range of formal and informal situations.

- monitor and adjust his/her own oral presentations to conform to selected criteria for acceptable performance.

4. The individual will independently

- use personal and objective criteria to assess the content, organization, and delivery of oral presentations designed for a general audience on a wide range of relevant personal and academic topics.

- express orally clear analyses and judgments of a range of issues, ideas, and experiences of general interest according to selected criteria.

- use clear language that reflects control of language conventions appropriate to a range of formal and informal situations.
- monitor and adjust his/her own oral presentations to conform to personally selected criteria for acceptable performance.

5. The individual will

- use, with direction, a limited range of personal and objective criteria to analyze and evaluate the content, organization, and delivery of oral communications on a limited variety of subjects.
- present oral analyses and evaluations of a limited range of issues, ideas, and experiences according to specific given criteria.
- use language and conventions appropriate to the subject and audience.
- monitor and evaluate his/her own performance as a speaker using given criteria.

6. The individual will

- use, without direction, a variety of personal and objective criteria to analyze and evaluate the content, organization, and delivery of oral communications on a wide variety of subjects.
- present oral analyses and evaluations of a wide range of issues, ideas, and experiences according to specific self- selected criteria.
- use language and conventions appropriate to the subject, the audience, and the context.
- monitor and evaluate his/her own performance as a speaker using self-selected personal and objective criteria.

7. The individual will

- select appropriate personal and objective criteria from a number of perspectives to evaluate the content, organization, and delivery of oral communications of considerable complexity and diversity on a wide variety of subjects and apply those criteria independently.
- present oral analyses and evaluations of diverse and complex issues ideas, and experiences according to self-selected criteria.
- use the language and conventions that most effectively persuade the audience of the validity of the evaluation.
- monitor and evaluate his/her own performance as a speaker according to the perceived needs and responses of the audience.

8. The individual will

- recognize the underlying assumptions and values by which he/she assesses complex oral communications and tolerates and accommodates a wide range of assessments based on assumptions and values that differ from his/her own and make judgments about the validity and applicability of criteria from diverse perspectives.
- present oral analyses and evaluations on complex issues, ideas, and experiences from diverse critical and cultural perspectives.
- use language creatively and individually for a desired effect.
- monitor and evaluate his/her own performance as a speaker with an awareness of the factors that influence audience attitudes toward a communication.

Pilot Study Participants

Teacher Researchers

Galen Boehme	Kinsley, Kansas
Sandra Jarvis Carey	Protection, Kansas
Crystal Cross	Great Bend, Kansas
Paul Feinstein	Buffalo, New York
Carol Forman-Pemberton	Burnt Hills, New York
Carol Gladstone	Bronx, New York
Patricia Hansbury-Zuendt	Guilderland, New York
Pamela Kissell	Fayetteville, New York
Joseph Quattrini	Canajoharie, New York
Carol Reynolds	Burnt Hills, New York
Mary Schwindt	Rozel, Kansas
Ruth Townsend	Yorktown Heights, New York
Nancy Zuwiyya	Binghamton, New York

Consultants/Reviewers

Brenda Randel	Great Bend, Kansas
Mary Sawyer	Albany, New York

References

Applebee, Arthur. 1978. *The Child's Concept of Story: Ages Two to Seventeen.* Chicago: The University of Chicago Press.

———. 1989. *A Study of Book-length Works Taught in High School English Courses.* Report Series 1.2. Albany: Center for the Learning and Teaching of Literature.

Atwell, Nancie. 1987. *In the Middle: Writing, Reading, and Learning with Adolescents.* Portsmouth, NH: Boynton/Cook Publishers.

Bakhtin, Mikhail. 1986. *Speech Genres and Other Late Essays.* Translated by Vern W. McGee. Edited by Caryl Emerson and Michael Holquist. Austin: University of Texas Press.

Barnes, Douglas, James Britton, and Mike Torbe. 1990. *Language, the Learner, and the School.* Portsmouth, NH: Heinemann Educational Books.

Bartholomae, David, and Anthony Petrosky. 1986. *Facts, Artifacts, and Counterfacts: Theory and Method for a Reading and Writing Course.* Upper Montclair, NJ: Boynton/Cook Publishers.

Berthoff, Ann E. 1978. *Forming, Thinking, Writing: The Composing Imagination.* Rochelle Park, NJ: Hayden Book Company.

———. 1981. *The Making of Meaning: Metaphors, Models, and Maxims for Writing Teachers.* Montclair, NJ: Boynton/Cook Publishers.

Boomer, Garth, ed. 1982. *Negotiating the Curriculum: A Teacher-Student Partnership.* Sydney: Ashton-Scholastic.

Boyer, Ernest L. 1981. *Common Learning: A Carnegie Colloquium on General Education.* Washington, DC: The Carnegie Foundation for the Advancement of Teaching.

———. 1983. *High School: A Report on Secondary Education in America.* New York: Harper & Row, Publishers.

Britton, James. 1970. *Language and Learning.* Coral Gables, FL: University of Miami Press.

———. 1982. *Prospect and Retrospect: Selected Essays.* Edited by Gordon M. Pradl. Portsmouth, NH: Boynton/Cook Publishers.

Bruner, Jerome. 1986. *Actual Minds, Possible Worlds.* Cambridge: Harvard University Press.

Cazden, Courtney. 1988. *Classroom Discourse.* Portsmouth, NH: Heinemann Educational Books.

Cooper, Charles R., and Lee Odell, eds. 1978. *Research on Composing: Points of Departure.* Urbana, IL: The National Council of Teachers of English.

Delpit, Lisa D. 1988a. "Language Diversity and Learning." In *Perspectives on Talk and Learning*, edited by Susan Hynds and Donald L. Rubin. Urbana, IL: The National Council of Teachers of English.

———. 1988b. "The Silenced Dialogue: Power and Pedagogy in Educating Other People's Children." *Harvard Educational Review* 58(August): 280–298.

Elbow, Peter. 1986. *Embracing Contraries: Explorations in Learning and Teaching*. New York: Oxford University Press.

———. 1990. *What Is English?* New York: The Modern Language Association of America and Urbana, IL: The National Council of Teachers of English.

———. 1991. "Reflections on Academic Discourse: How It Relates to Freshmen and Colleagues." *College English* 53 (February): 135–155.

Eliot, T. S. 1971. *Four Quartets*. New York: Harcourt Brace Jovanovich, Inc.

Fetterley, Judith. 1978. *The Resisting Reader: A Feminist Approach to American Fiction*. Bloomington: Indiana University Press.

Freire, Paulo. 1987. "Letter to North American Teachers." Translated by Carman Hunter. In *Freire for the Classroom: A Sourcebook for Liberatory Teaching*, edited by Ira Shor. Portsmouth, NH: Boynton/Cook Publishers.

Frye, Northrop. 1957. *Anatomy of Criticism: Four Essays*. Princeton, NJ: Princeton University Press.

Gardner, Howard. 1983. *Frames of Mind: The Theory of Multiple Intelligences*. New York: Basic Books.

Goodlad, John I. 1984. *A Place Called School: Prospects for the Future*. New York: McGraw-Hill.

Grant Commission on Work, Family, and Citizenship. 1988. *The Forgotten Half: Pathways to Success for America's Youth and Young Families*. Washington, DC: Grant Commission.

Halliday, Michael A. K. 1973. *Explorations in the Functions of Language*. London: Edward Arnold.

———. 1978. *Language as Social Semiotic: The Social Interpretation of Language and Meaning*. Baltimore: University Park Press.

Heath, Shirley Brice. 1983a. "A Lot of Talk about Nothing." *Language Arts* 60, no. 8 (November/December).

———. 1983b. *Ways with Words: Language, Life, and Work in Communities and Classrooms*. New York: Cambridge University Press.

Hirsch, E. D. 1987. *Cultural Literacy: What Every American Needs to Know*. Boston: Houghton Mifflin.

Iser, Wolfgang. 1980. "The Reading Process: A Phenomenological Approach." In *Reader-Response Criticism: From Formalism to Post-Structuralism*, edited by J. P. Tompkins. Baltimore: The Johns Hopkins University Press.

Ishiguro, Kazuo. 1989. *The Remains of the Day*. New York: Vintage Books.

Johnston, Peter H. 1992. *Constructive Evaluation of Literate Activity*. New York: Longman Publishing Group.

Langer, Suzanne. 1930. *The Practice of Philosophy*. New York: Holt.

Marshall, James. 1988. "Classroom Discourse and Literary Response." In *Literature in the Classroom: Readers, Texts, and Contexts*, edited by B. Nelms. Urbana, IL: The National Council of Teachers of English.

Mayher, John S. 1990. *Uncommon Sense: Theoretical Practice in Language Education*. Portsmouth, NH: Heinemann Educational Books.

Michaels, S., and Courtney Cazden. 1986. "Teacher-Child Collaboration as Oral Preparation for Literacy." In *Acquisition of Literacy: Ethnographic Perspectives*, edited by B. Schieffer. Norwood, NJ: Ablex.

Moffett, James. 1970. "Misbehaviorist English: A Position Paper." In *On Writing Behavioral Objectives for English*, edited by J. Maxwell and A. Tovatt. Urbana, IL: The National Council of Teachers of English.

Naisbitt, J., and Patricia Aburdene. 1986. *Re-inventing the Corporation*. New York: Warner Books.

Odell, Lee. 1977. "Measuring Changes in Intellectual Processes as One Dimension of Growth in Writing." In *Evaluating Writing: Describing, Measuring, Judging*, edited by C. R. Cooper and L. Odell. Urbana, IL: The National Council of Teachers of English.

———. 1989. Presentation at the State Education Department Conference, "Improving Writing: An Ongoing Process." Albany, NY.

Ostriker, Alicia. 1985. "The Thieves of Language: Women Poets and Revisionist Mythmaking." In *The New Feminist Criticism: Essays on Women, Literature, and Theory*, edited by E. Showalter. New York: Pantheon Books.

Probst, Robert. 1988. *Response and Analysis: Teaching Literature in Junior and Senior High School*. Portsmouth, NH: Heinemann Educational Books.

Purves, Alan C. 1985. "That Sunny Dome: Those Caves of Ice." In *Researching Response to Literature and the Teaching of Literature: Points of Departure*, edited by C. R. Cooper. Norwood, NJ: Ablex Publishing.

———. 1988. "Literacy as Common Knowledge and Conventional Wisdom." Paper presented at the First Gutenberg Conference. Albany: Center for Writing and Literacy.

Purves, Alan C., Theresa Rogers, and Anna O. Soter. 1990. *How Porcupines Make Love II: Teaching a Response-Centered Literature Curriculum*. New York: Longman Publishing.

Rose, Mike. 1989. *Lives on the Boundary: A Moving Account of the Struggles and Achievements of America's Educational Underclass*. New York: Penguin Books.

Rosenblatt, Louise M. 1978. *The Reader, the Text, the Poem: The Transactional Theory of the Literary Work*. Carbondale: Southern Illinois University Press.

———. 1983. *Literature as Exploration*. New York: Modern Language Association of America.

————. 1989. "Writing and Reading: The Transactional Theory." In *Reading and Writing Connections*. Edited by J. M. Mason. Boston: Allyn & Bacon.

Santiago-Santiago, Isaura. 1989. Presentation to Brooklyn Reading Council.

Scholes, Robert. 1985. *Textual Power: Literary Theory and the Teaching of English*. New Haven: Yale University Press.

The Secretary's Commission on Achieving Necessary Skills (SCANS). 1991. *What Work Requires of Schools: A SCANS Report for America 2000*. Washington, DC: U. S. Department of Labor.

Slevin, James F. 1988. "Genre Theory, Academic Discourse, and Writing Within Disciplines." In *Audits of Meaning: A Festschrift in Honor of Ann E. Berthoff*, edited by L. Z. Smith. Portsmouth, NH: Heinemann Educational Books.

Smith, Frank. 1988. *Joining the Literacy Club: Further Essays into Education*. Portsmouth, NH: Heinemann Educational Books.

Squire, James R., and Roger K. Applebee. 1968. *High School English Instruction Today*. New York: Appleton-Century-Crofts.

Tierney, Robert. J., Mark A. Carter, and Laura E. Desai. 1991. *Portfolio Assessment in the Reading-Writing Classroom*. Norwood, MA: Christopher-Gordon Publishers, Inc.

Vygotsky, Lev S. 1962. *Thought and Language*. Cambridge: MIT Press.

White, Hayden. 1985. *Tropics of Discourse: Essays in Cultural Criticism*. Baltimore: The Johns Hopkins University Press.

Wolf, Dennie Palmer, Janet Bixby, John Glenn III, and Howard Gardner. 1991. "To Use Their Minds Well: Investigating New Forms of Student Assessment." In *Review of Research in Education*, edited by G. Grant. Washington: American Educational Research Association.

Zemelman, Steven, and Harvey Daniels. 1988. *A Community of Writers: Teaching Writing in the Junior and Senior High School*. Portsmouth, NH: Heinemann Educational Books.

Index

Aburdene, Patricia, 159
academic discourse, 14. *See also* disciplinary discourse
  conventions in, 37
  student understanding of, 24–25
adult-level performance, 68, 70, 75
aesthetic response and expression, 5–11, 19
  across the curriculum, 124–25
  exit outcomes, 112
  flexibility in, 28–29
  focusing narrative report around, 106
  lack of attention to, 7
  language experiences, 115–25, 144
  listening, 6–9, 50–52, 186–88
    in English class, 121–24
  range in, 23–24
  reading, 6–9, 47–49, 64, 170–72
    in English class, 117–21
    performance continuum, 47–49, 64
    range and, 23
    vs. efferent reading, 9, 23
  speaking, 9–11, 50–52, 186–88
    in English class, 121–24
  vs. information and understanding, 13
  writing, 9–11, 49–50, 176–78
    cultural diversity and, 150–51
    in English class, 115–17
    performance continuum, 49–50, 65
analysis. *See* critical analysis
analytical language, 13
Anatomy of Criticism (Frye), 36
Applebee, Arthur, 152–53
assessment scales, resistance to, 43–44

assessment. *See* classroom assessment; outcomes assessment; performance continuum
Atwell, Nancie, 130, 132, 141
audience
  feedback from, 130
  writing for, 10–11, 127–28
authority
  academic discourse and, 37
  aesthetic reading and, 48
  informational language and, 13–14, 24–25
  through writing, 115–16

Barnes, Douglas, 121
Bartholomae, David, 14, 34, 37, 129, 130
benchmarks
  defined, 71–72, 86
  for elementary performance, 72, 73
  for intermediate performance, 74
Berthoff, Ann, 21, 40, 129, 136
Bleich, David, 7
Boehme, Galen, 105
Boomer, Garth, 131
Boyer, Ernest, 113
Britton, James, 5–6, 13, 14, 15, 17, 18, 27, 31, 121, 134–35, 142, 143

Carnegie Foundation, 113
Cazden, Courtney, 151
characteristics of performance, 21–42. *See also* performance; performance continuum
  connections, 21, 32–35, 41
  conventions, 21, 35–38, 41–42
  flexibility, 21, 28–32, 41
  independence, 21, 39–40, 42
  range, 21, 22–28, 41
cheating, 39